CONVERSATIONS AND DIALOGUES-II

By

SWAMI VIVEKANANDA

CONVERSATIONS AND DIALOGUES-II
by SWAMI VIVEKANANDA

ISBN: 978-93-59393-62-9

Published by

DOUBLE 9 BOOKS

2/13-B, Ansari Road, Daryaganj
New Delhi – 110002
info@double9books.com
www.double9books.com
Tel. 011-40042856

ABOUT THE AUTHOR

Swami Vivekananda was born Narendranath Datta in India on January 12, 1863. He died on July 4, 1902, and was the most important student of the Indian saint Ramakrishna. He was an important part of bringing Vedanta and Yoga to the West. He is also charged with making people more aware of other religions and making Hinduism a major world religion. Vivekananda had a lot of success at the Parliament. In the years that followed, he gave hundreds of lectures across the United States, England, and Europe to spread the main ideas of Hinduism. He also started the Vedanta Society of New York and the Vedanta Society of San Francisco, which is now the Vedanta Society of Northern California. Both of these groups became the basis for Vedanta Societies in the West. Vivekananda was one of the most important philosophers and social reformers in India at the time. He was also one of the most successful and powerful Vedanta missionaries in the West.People now think of him as one of the most important people in modern India and Hinduism. Mahatma Gandhi said that after reading Vivekananda's works, he loved his country a thousand times more.

CONTENTS

I

(*Translated from Bengali*)

(*From the Diary of a Disciple*)

(The disciple is Sharatchandra Chakravarty, who published his records in a Bengali book, *Swami-Shishya-Samvâda*, in two parts. The present series of "Conversations and Dialogues" is a revised translation from this book. Five dialogues of this series have already appeared in the *Complete Works*, Vol. V.)

[Place: Calcutta, the house of the late Babu Priyanath Mukhopadhyaya, Baghbazar. Year: 1897.]

It is three or four days since Swamiji has set his foot in Calcutta (On February 20, 1897.) after his first return from the West. The joy of the devotees of Shri Ramakrishna knows no bounds at enjoying his holy presence after a long time. And the well-to-do among them are considering themselves blessed to cordially invite Swamiji to their own houses. This afternoon Swamiji had an invitation to the house of Srijut Priyanath Mukhopadhyaya, a devotee of Shri Ramakrishna, at Rajballabhpara in Baghbazar. Receiving this news, many devotees assembled today in his house.

The disciple also, informed of it through indirect sources, reached the house of Mr. Mukherjee at about 2-30 p.m. He had not yet made his acquaintance with Swamiji. So this was to be his first meeting with the Swami.

On the disciple's reaching there, Swami Turiyananda took him to Swamiji and introduced him. After his return to the Math, the Swami had already heard about him, having read a Hymn on Shri Ramakrishna composed by the disciple.

Swamiji also had come to know that the disciple used to visit Nâg Mahâshaya, a foremost devotee of Shri Ramakrishna.

When the disciple prostrated himself before him and took his seat, Swamiji addressed him in Sanskrit and asked him about Nag Mahashaya and his health, and while referring to his superhuman renunciation, his unbounded love for God, and his humility, he said:

"वयं तत्त्वान्वेषात् हता मधुकर त्वं खलु कृती ।

(Words addressed by King Dushyanta to the bee which was teasing Shakuntalâ by darting at her lips — Kalidasa's *Shâkuntalam*.)

— "We are undone by our vain quest after reality; while, O bee, you are indeed blessed with success!" He then asked the disciple to send these words to Nag Mahashaya. Afterwards, finding it rather inconvenient to talk to the disciple in the crowd, he called him and Swami Turiyananda to a small room to the west and, addressing himself to the disciple, began to recite these words from the *Vivekachudâmani* (43):

"मा भैष्ट विद्वंस्तव नास्त्यपायः
संसारसिन्धोस्तरणेऽस्त्युपायः ।
येनैव याता यतयोऽस्य पारं
तमेव मार्गं तव निर्दिशामि ॥

— "O wise one, fear not; you have not to perish. Means there are for crossing the ocean of this round of birth and death. I shall show you the same way by which holy men of renunciation have crossed this ocean." He then asked him to read Âchârya Shankara's work named *Vivekachudâmani*.

At these words, the disciple went on musing within himself. Was the Swami in this way hinting at the desirability of his own formal initiation? The disciple was at that time a staunch orthodox man in his ways, and a Vedantin. He had not yet settled his mind as regards the adoption of a Guru and was a devoted advocate of Varnâshrama or caste ordinances.

While various topics were going on, a man came in and announced that Mr. Narendranath Sen, the Editor of the *Mirror*, had come for an interview with Swamiji. Swamiji asked the bearer of this news to show him into that small room. Narendra Babu came and taking a seat there introduced various topics about England and America. In answer to his questions Swamiji said, "Nowhere in the world is to be found another nation like the Americans, so generous, broad-minded, hospitable, and so sincerely eager to accept new ideas." "Wherever work", he went on, "has been done in America has not been done through my power. The people of America have accepted the ideas of Vedanta, because they are so good-hearted." Referring to England he said, "There is no nation in the world so conservative as the English. They do not like so easily to accept any new idea, but if through perseverance they can be once made to understand any idea, they will never give it up by any means. Such firm determination you will find in no other nation. This is why they occupy the foremost position in the world in power and civilization."

Then declaring that if qualified preachers could be had, there was greater likelihood of the Vedanta work being permanently established in England than in America, he continued, "I have only laid the foundation of the work. If future preachers follow my path, a good deal of work may be done in time."

Narendra Babu asked, "What future prospect is there for us in preaching religion in this way?"

Swamiji said: "In our country there is only this religion of Vedanta. Compared with the Western civilisation, it may be said, we have hardly got anything else. But by the preaching of this universal religion of Vedanta, a religion which gives equal rights to acquire spirituality to men of all creeds and all paths of religious practice, the civilised West would come to know what a wonderful degree of spirituality once developed in India and how that is still existing. By the study of this religion, the Western nations will have increasing regard and sympathy for us. Already these have grown to some extent. In this way, if we have their real sympathy and regard, we would learn from them the sciences bearing on our material life, thereby qualifying ourselves better for the struggle for existence. On the other hand, by learning this Vedanta from us, they will be enabled to secure their own spiritual welfare."

Narendra Babu asked, "Is there any hope of our political progress in this kind of interchange?"

Swamiji said, "They (the Westerners) are the children of the great hero Virochana! Their power makes the five elements play like puppets in their hands. If you people believe that we shall in case of conflict with them gain freedom by applying those material forces, you are profoundly mistaken. Just as a little piece of stone figures before the Himalayas, so we differ from them in point of skill in the use of those forces. Do you know what my idea is? By preaching the profound secrets of the Vedanta religion in the Western world, we shall attract the sympathy and regard of these mighty nations, maintaining for ever the position of their teacher in spiritual matters, and they will remain our teachers in all material concerns. The day when, surrendering the spiritual into their hands, our countrymen would sit at the feet of the West to learn religion, that day indeed the nationality of this fallen nation will be dead and gone for good. Nothing will come of crying day and night before them, 'Give me this or give me that.' When there will grow a link of sympathy and regard between both nations by this give-and-take intercourse, there will be then no need for these noisy cries. They will do everything of their own accord. I believe that by this cultivation of religion and the wider diffusion of Vedanta, both this country and the West will gain enormously. To me the pursuit of politics is a secondary means in comparison with this. I will lay down my life to carry out this belief practically. If you believe in any other way of accomplishing the good of India, well, you may go on working your own way."

Narendra Babu shortly left, expressing his unqualified agreement with Swamiji's ideas. The disciple, hearing the above words from Swamiji, astonishingly contemplated his luminous features with steadfast gaze.

When Narendra Babu had departed, an enthusiastic preacher belonging to the society for the protection of cows came for an interview with Swamiji. He was dressed almost like a Sannyasin, if not fully so — with a Geruâ turban on the head; he was evidently an up-country Indian. At the announcement of this preacher of cow-protection Swamiji came out to the parlour room. The preacher saluted Swamiji and presented him with a picture of the mother-cow. Swamiji took that in his hand and, making it over to one standing by, commenced the following conversation with the preacher:

Swamiji: What is the object of your society?

Preacher: We protect the mother-cows of our country from the hands of the butcher. Cow-infirmaries have been founded in some places where the diseased, decrepit mother-cows or those bought from the butchers are provided for.

Swamiji: That is very good indeed. What is the source of your income?

Preacher: The work of the society is carried on only by gifts kindly made by great men like you.

Swamiji: What amount of money have you now laid by?

Preacher: The Marwari traders' community are the special supporters of this work. They have given a big amount for this good cause.

Swamiji: A terrible famine has now broken out in Central India. The Indian Government has published a death-roll of nine lakhs of starved people. Has your society done anything to render help in this time of famine?

Preacher: We do not help during famine or other distresses. This society has been established only for the protection of mother-cows.

Swamiji: During a famine when lakhs of people, your own brothers and sisters, have fallen into the jaws of death, you have not thought it your duty, though having the means, to help them in that terrible calamity with food!

Preacher: No. This famine broke out as a result of men's Karma, their sins. It is a case of "like Karma, like fruit".

Hearing the words of the preacher, sparks of fire, as it were, scintillated in Swamiji's large eyes; his face became flushed. But he suppressed his feeling and said: "Those associations which do not feel sympathy for men and, even seeing their own brothers dying from starvation, do not give them a handful of rice to save their lives, while giving away piles of food to save birds and beasts, I have not the least sympathy for, and I do not believe that society derives any good from them. If you make a plea of Karma by saying that men die through their Karma, then it becomes a settled fact that it is useless to try or struggle for anything in this world; and your work for the protection of animals is no exception. With regard to your cause also, it can be said — the mother-cows through their own Karma fall into the hands of the butchers and die, and we need not do anything in the matter."

The preacher was a little abashed and said: "Yes, what you say is true, but the Shâstras say that the cow is our mother."

Swamiji smilingly said, "Yes, that the cow is our mother, I understand: who else could give birth to *such* accomplished children?"

The up-country preacher did not speak further on the subject; perhaps he could not understand the point of Swamiji's poignant ridicule. He told Swamiji that he was begging something of him for the objects of the society.

Swamiji: I am a Sannyasin, a fakir. Where shall I find money enough to help you? But if ever I get money in my possession, I shall first spend that in the service of man. Man is first to be saved; he must be given food, education, and spirituality. If any money is left after doing all these, then only something would be given to your society.

At these words, the preacher went away after saluting Swamiji. Then Swamiji began to speak to us: "What words, these, forsooth! Says he that men are dying by reason of their Karma, so what avails doing any kindness to them! This is decisive proof that the country has gone to rack and ruin! Do you see how much abused the Karma theory of your Hinduism has been? Those who are men and yet have no feeling in the heart for man, well, are such to be counted as men at all?" While speaking these words, Swamiji's whole body seemed to shiver in anguish and grief.

Then, while smoking, Swamiji said to the disciple, "Well, see me again."

Disciple: Where will you be staying, sir? Perhaps you might put up in some rich man's house. Will he allow me there?

Swamiji: At present, I shall be living either at the Alambazar Math or at the garden-house of Gopal Lal Seal at Cossipore. You may come to either place.

Disciple: Sir, I very much wish to speak with you in solitude.

Swamiji: All right. Come one night. We shall speak plenty of Vedanta.

Disciple: Sir, I have heard that some Europeans and Americans have come with you. Will they not get offended at my dress or my talk?

Swamiji: Why, they are also men, and moreover they are devoted to the Vedanta religion. They will be glad to converse with you.

Disciple: Sir, Vedanta speaks of some distinctive qualifications for its aspirants; how could these come out in your Western disciples? The Shastras say — he who has studied the Vedas and the Vedanta, who has formally expiated his sins, who has performed all the daily and occasional duties enjoined by the scriptures, who is self-restrained in his food and general conduct, and specially he who is accomplished in the four special Sâdhanâs (preliminary disciplines), he alone has a right to the practice of Vedanta. Your Western disciples are in the first place non-Brahmins, and then they are lax in point of proper food and dress; how could they understand the system of Vedanta?

Swamiji: When you speak with them, you will know at once whether they have understood Vedanta or not.

Swamiji, perhaps, could now see that the disciple was rigidly devoted to the external observances of orthodox Hinduism. Swamiji then, surrounded by some devotees of Shri Ramakrishna, went over to the house of Srijut Balaram Basu of Baghbazar. The disciple bought the book *Vivekachudamani* at Bat-tala and went towards his own home at Darjipara.

II

(Translated from Bengali)

(From the Diary of a Disciple)

(The disciple is Sharatchandra Chakravarty, who published his records in a Bengali book, *Swami-Shishya-Samvâda*, in two parts. The present series of "Conversations and Dialogues" is a revised translation from this book. Five dialogues of this series have already appeared in the *Complete Works*, Vol. V.)

[Place: On the way from Calcutta to Cossipore and in the garden of the late Gopal Lal Seal. Year: 1897.]

Today Swamiji was taking rest at noon in the house of Srijut Girish Chandra Ghosh. The disciple arriving there saluted him and found that Swamiji was just ready to go to the garden-house of Gopal Lal Seal. A carriage was waiting outside. He said to the disciple, "Well come with me." The disciple agreeing, Swamiji got up with him into the carriage and it started. When it drove up the Chitpur road, on seeing the Gangâ, Swamiji broke forth in a chant, self-involved: "गङ्गातरङ्ग-रमणीय-जटा-कलापं" etc. The disciple listened in silent wonder to that wave of music, when after a short while, seeing a railway engine going towards the Chitpur hydraulic bridge, Swamiji said to the disciple, "Look how it goes majestically like a lion! " The disciple replied, "But that is inert matter. Behind it there is the intelligence of man working, and hence it moves. In moving thus, what credit is there for it?"

Swamiji: Well, say then, what is the sign of consciousness?

Disciple: Why, sir, that indeed is conscious which acts through intelligence.

Swamiji: Everything is conscious which rebels against nature: there, consciousness is manifested. Just try to kill a little ant, even it will once resist to save its life. Where there is struggle, where there is rebellion, there is the sign of life, there consciousness is manifested.

Disciple: Sir, can that test be applied also in the case of men and of nations?

Swamiji: Just read the history of the world and see whether it applies or not. You will find that excepting yours, it holds good in the case of all other nations. It is you only who are in this world lying prostrate today like inert matter. You have been hypnotised. From very old times, others have been telling you that you are weak, that you have no power, and you also, accepting that, have for about a thousand years gone on thinking, "We are wretched, we are good for nothing." (Pointing to his own body:) This body also is born of the soil of your country; but I never thought like that. And hence you see how, through His will, even those who always think us low and weak, have done and are still doing me divine honour. If you can think that infinite power, infinite knowledge and indomitable energy lie within you, and if you can bring out that power, you also can become like me.

Disciple: Where is the capacity in us for thinking that way, sir? Where is the teacher or preceptor who from our childhood will speak thus before us and make us understand? What we have heard and have learnt from all is that the object of having an education nowadays is to secure some good job.

Swamiji: For that reason is it that we have come forward with quite another precept and example. Learn that truth from us, understand it, and realise it and then spread that idea broadcast, in cities, in towns, and in villages. Go and preach to all, "Arise, awake, sleep no more; within each of you there is the power to remove all wants and all miseries. Believe this, and that power will be manifested." Teach this to all, and, with that, spread among the masses in plain language the central truths of science, philosophy, history, and geography. I have a plan to open a centre with the unmarried youths; first of all I shall teach them, and then carry on the work through them.

Disciple: But that requires a good deal of money. Where will you get this money?

Swamiji: What do you talk! Isn't it man that makes moneys Where did you ever hear of money making man? If you can make your thoughts and words perfectly at one, if you can, I say, make yourself one in speech and action, money will pour in at your feet of itself, like water.

Disciple: Well, sir, I take it for granted that money will come, and you will begin that good work. But what will that matter? Before this, also, many great men carried out many good deeds. But where are they now? To be sure, the same fate awaits the work which you are going to start. Then what is the good of such an endeavour?

Swamiji: He who always speculates as to what awaits him in future, accomplishes nothing whatsoever. What you have understood as true and good, just do that at once. What's the good of calculating what may or may not befall in future? The span of life is so, so short — and can anything be accomplished in it if you go on forecasting and computing results. God is the only dispenser of results; leave it to Him to do all that. What have you got to do with on working.

While he was thus going on, the cab reached the gardenhouse. Many people from Calcutta came to the garden that day to see Swamiji. Swamiji got down from the carriage, took his seat in the room, and began conversation with them all. Mr. Goodwin, a Western disciple of Swamiji, was standing near by, like the embodiment of service, as it were. The disciple had already made his acquaintance; so he came to Mr. Goodwin, and both engaged in a variety of talk about Swamiji.

In the evening Swamiji called the disciple and asked him, "Have you got the Katha Upanishad by heart?"

Disciple: No, sir, I have only read it with Shankara's commentary.

Swamiji: Among the Upanishads, one finds no other book so beautiful as this. I wish you would all get it by heart. What will it do only to read it? Rather try to bring into your life the faith, the courage, the discrimination, and the renunciation of Nachiketâ.

Disciple: Give your blessings, please, that I may realise these.

Swamiji: You have heard of Shri Ramakrishna's words, haven't you? He used to say, "The breeze of mercy is already blowing, do you only hoist the sail." Can anybody, my boy, thrust realization upon another? One's destiny is in one's own hands — the Guru only makes this much understood. Through the power of the seed itself the tree grows, the air and water are only aids.

Disciple: There is, sir, the necessity also of extraneous help.

Swamiji: Yes, there is. But you should know that if there be no substance within, no amount of outside help will avail anything. Yet there comes a time for everyone to realise the Self. For everyone is Brahman. The distinction of higher and lower is only in the degree of manifestation of that Brahman. In time, everyone will have perfect manifestation. Hence the Shâstras say, "कालेनात्मनि विन्दति — In time, That is realised in one's self."

Disciples When, alas, will that happen, sir? From the Shastras we hear how many births we have had to pass in ignorance!

Swamiji: What's the fear? When you have come here this time, the goal shall be attained in this life. Liberation or Samâdhi — all this consists in simply doing away with the obstacles to the manifestation of Brahman. Otherwise the Self is always shining forth like the sun. The cloud of ignorance has only veiled it. Remove the cloud and the sun will manifest. Then you get into the state of "भिद्यते हृदयग्रन्थिः" ("the knot of the heart is broken") etc. The various paths that you find, all advise you to remove the obstacles on the way. The way by which one realises the Self, is the way which he preached to all. But the goal of all is the knowledge of the Self, the realization of this Self. To it all men, all beings have equal right. This is the view acceptable to all.

Disciple: Sir, when I read or hear these words of the Shastras, the thought that the Self has not yet been realised makes the heart very disconsolate.

Swamiji: This is what is called longing. The more it grows the more will the cloud of obstacles be dispelled, and stronger will faith be established. Gradually the Self will be realised like a fruit on the palm of one's hand. This realisation alone is the soul of religion. Everyone can go on abiding by some observances and formalities. Everyone can fulfil certain injunctions and prohibitions but how few have this longing for realization! This intense longing — becoming mad after realising God or getting the knowledge of the Self — is real spirituality. The irresistible madness which the Gopis had for the Lord, Shri Krishna, yea, it is intense longing like that which is necessary for the realization of the Self! Even in the Gopis' mind there was a slight distinction of man and woman. But in real Self-knowledge, there is not the slightest distinction of sex.

While speaking thus, Swamiji introduced the subject of *Gita-Govindam* (of Jayadeva) and continued saying:

Jayadeva was the last poet in Sanskrit literature though he often cared more for the jingling of words than for depth of sentiment. But just see how the poet has shown the culmination of love and longing in the Shloka "पतति पतत्रे" etc. Such love indeed is necessary for Self-realisation. There must be fretting and pining within the heart. Now from His playful life at Vrindaban come to the Krishna of Kurukshetra, and see how that also is fascinating — how, amidst all that horrible din and uproar of fighting, Krishna remains calm, balanced, and peaceful. Ay, on the very battlefield, He is speaking the Gita to Arjuna and getting him on to fight, which is the Dharma of a Kshatriya! Himself an agent to bring about this terrible warfare, Shri Krishna remains unattached to action — He did not take up arms! To whichsoever phase of it you look, you will find the character of Shri Krishna perfect. As if He was the embodiment of knowledge, work, devotion, power of concentration, and everything! In the present age, this aspect of Shri Krishna should be specially studied. Only contemplating the Krishna of Vrindaban with His flute won't do nowadays — that will not bring salvation to humanity. Now is needed the worship of Shri Krishna uttering forth the lion-roar of the Gita, of Râma with His bow and arrows, of Mahâvira, of Mother Kâli. Then only will the people grow strong by going to work with great energy and will. I have considered the matter most carefully and come to the conclusion that of those who profess and talk of religion nowadays in this country, the majority are full of morbidity — crack-brained or fanatic. Without development of an abundance of Rajas, you have hopes neither in this world, nor in the next. The whole country is enveloped in intense Tamas; and naturally the result is — servitude in this life and hell in the next.

Disciple: Do you expect in view of the Rajas in the Westerners that they will gradually become Sâttvika?

Swamiji: Certainly. Possessed of a plenitude of Rajas, they have now reached the culmination of Bhoga, or enjoyment. Do you think that it is not they, but you, who are going to achieve Yoga — you who hang about for the sake of your bellies? At the sight of their highly refined enjoyment, the delineation in *Meghaduta* " विद्युद्दन्तं ललितवसना:" — etc. — comes to my mind. And your Bhoga consists in lying on a ragged bed in a muggy room, multiplying progeny every year like a hog! — Begetting a band of famished beggars and slaves! Hence do I say, let people be made energetic and active in nature by the stimulation of Rajas. Work, work, work; " नान्यः पन्था विद्यतेऽयनाय — There is no other path of liberation but this."

Disciple: Sir, did our forefathers possess this kind of Rajas?

Swamiji: Why, did they not? Does not history tell us that they established colonies in many countries, and sent preachers of religion to Tibet, China, Sumatra, and even to far-off Japan? Do you think there is any other means of achieving progress except through Rajas?

As conversation thus went on, night approached; and meanwhile Miss Müller came there. She was an English lady, having great reverence for Swamiji. Swamiji introduced the disciple to her, and after a short talk Miss Müller went upstairs.

Swamiji: See, to what a heroic nation they belong! How far-off is her home, and she is the daughter of a rich man — yet how long a way has she come, only with the hope of realising the spiritual ideal!

Disciple: Yes, sir, but your works are stranger still! How so many Western ladies and gentlemen are always eager to serve you! For this age, it is very strange indeed!

Swamiji: If this body lasts, you will see many more things. If I can get some young men of heart and energy, I shall revolutionize the whole country. There are a few in Madras. But I have more hope in Bengal. Such clear brains are to be found scarcely in any other country. But they have no strength in their muscles. The brain and muscles must develop simultaneously. Iron nerves with an intelligent brain — and the whole world is at your feet.

Word was brought that supper was ready for Swamiji. He said to the disciple, "Come and have a look at my food." While going on with the supper, he said, "It is not good to take much fatty or oily substance. Roti is better than Luchi. Luchi is the food of the sick. Take fish and meat and fresh vegetables, but sweets sparingly." While thus talking, he inquired, "Well, how many Rotis have I taken? Am I to take more? He did not remember how much he took and did not feel even it he yet had any appetite. The sense of body faded away so much while he was talking!

He finished after taking a little more. The disciple also took leave and went back to Calcutta. Getting no cab for hire, he had to walk; and while walking, he thought over in his mind how soon again he could come the next day to see Swamiji.

III

(Translated from Bengali)
(From the Diary of a Disciple)

(The disciple is Sharatchandra Chakravarty, who published his records in a Bengali book, *Swami-Shishya-Samvâda*, in two parts. The present series of "Conversations and Dialogues" is a revised translation from this book. Five dialogues of this series have already appeared in the *Complete Works*, Vol. V.)

[Place: Cossipore, at the garden of the late Gopal Lal Seal. Year: 1897.]

After his first return from the West, Swamiji resided for a few days at the garden of the late Gopal Lal Seal at Cossipore. Some well-known Pundits living at Barabazar, Calcutta, came to the garden one day with a view to holding a disputation with him. The disciple was present there on the occasion.

All the Pundits who came there could speak in Sanskrit fluently. They came and greeting Swamiji, who sat surrounded by a circle of visitors, began their conversation in Sanskrit. Swamiji also responded to them in melodious Sanskrit. The disciple cannot remember now the subject on which the Pundits argued with him that day. But this much he remembers that the Pundits, almost all in one strident voice, were rapping out to Swamiji in Sanskrit subtle questions of philosophy, and he, in a dignified serious mood, was giving out to them calmly his own well argued conclusions about those questions.

In the discussion with the Pundits Swamiji represented the side of the Siddhânta or conclusions to be established, while the Pundits represented that of the Purvapaksha or objections to be raised. The disciple remembers that, while arguing, Swamiji wrongly used in one place the word Asti instead of Svasti, which made the Pundits laugh out. At this, Swamiji at once submitted: " पण्डितानां दासोऽहं क्षन्तव्यमेतत् स्खलनम् — I am but a servant of the Pundits, please excuse this mistake." The Pundits also were charmed at this humility of Swamiji. After a long dispute, the Pundits at last admitted that the conclusions of the Siddhanta side were adequate, and preparing to depart, they made their greetings to Swamiji.

After the Pundits had left, the disciple learnt from Swamiji that these Pundits who took the side of the Purvapaksha were well versed in the Purva-Mimâmsâ Shâstras, Swamiji advocated the philosophy of the Uttara-Mimâmsâ or Vedanta and proved to them the superiority of the path of knowledge, and they were obliged to accept his conclusions.

About the way the Pundits laughed at Swamiji, picking up one grammatical mistake, he said that this error of his was due to the fact of his not having spoken in Sanskrit for many years together. He did not blame the Pundits a bit for all that. But he pointed out in this connection that in the West it would imply a great incivility on the part of an opponent to point out any such slip in language, deviating from the real issue of dispute. A civilised society in such cases would accept the idea, taking no notice of the language. "But in your country, all the fighting is going on over the husk, nobody searches for the kernel within." So saying, Swamiji began to talk with the disciple in Sanskrit. The disciple also gave answers in broken Sanskrit. Yet Swamiji praised him for the sake of encouragement. From that day, at the request of Swamiji, the disciple used to speak with him in Sanskrit off and on.

In reply to the question, what is civilisation, Swamiji said that day: "The more advanced a society or nation is in spirituality, the more is that society or nation civilised. No nation can be said to have become civilised only because it has succeeded in increasing the comforts of material life by bringing into use lots of machinery and things of that sort. The present-day civilization of the West is multiplying day by day only the wants and distresses of men. On the other hand, the ancient Indian civilisation by showing people the way to spiritual advancement, doubtless succeeded, if not in removing once for all, at least in lessening, in a great measure, the material needs of men. In the present age, it is to bring into coalition both these civilisations that Bhagavan Shri Ramakrishna was born. In this age, as on the one hand people have to be intensely practical, so on the other hand they have to acquire deep spiritual knowledge." Swamiji made us clearly understand that day that from such interaction of the Indian civilization with that of the West would dawn on the world a new era. In the course of dilating upon this, he happened to remark in one place, "Well, another thing. People there in the West think that the more a man is religious, the more demure he must be in his outward bearing — no word about anything else from his lips! As the priests in the West would on the one hand be struck with wonder at my liberal religious discourses, they would be as much puzzled on the other hand when they found me, after such discourses, talking frivolities with my friends. Sometimes they would speak out to my face: 'Swami, you are a priest, you should not be joking and laughing in this way like ordinary men. Such levity does not look well in you.' To which I would reply, 'We are children of bliss, why should we look morose and sombre?' But I doubt if they could rightly catch the drift of my words."

That day Swamiji spoke many things about Bhâva Samâdhi and Nirvikalpa Samadhi as well. These are produced below as far as possible:

Suppose a man is cultivating that type of devotion to God which Hanumân represents. The more intense the attitude becomes, the more will the pose and demeanour of that aspirant, nay even his physical configuration, be cast in that would. It is in this way that transmutation of species takes place. Taking up any such emotional attitude, the worshipper becomes gradually shaped into the very form of his ideal. The ultimate stage of any such sentiment is called Bhava Samadhi. While the aspirant in the path of Jnana, pursuing the process of Neti, Neti, "not this, not this", such as "I am not the body, nor the mind, nor the intellect", and so on, attains to the Nirvikalpa Samadhi when he is established in absolute consciousness. It requires striving through many births to reach perfection or the ultimate stage with regard to a single one of these devotional attitudes. But Shri Ramakrishna, the king of the realm of spiritual sentiment, perfected himself in no less than eighteen different forms of devotion! He also used to say that his body would not have endured, had he not held himself on to this play of spiritual sentiment.

The disciple asked that day, "Sir, what sort of food did you use to take in the West?"

Swamiji: The same as they take there. We are Sannyasins and nothing can take away our caste!

On the subject of how he would work in future in this country, Swamiji said that day that starting two centres, one in Madras and another in Calcutta, he would rear up a new type of Sannyasins for the good of all men in all its phases. He further said that by a destructive method no progress either for the society or for the country could be achieved. In all ages and times progress has been effected by the constructive process, that is, by giving a new mould to old methods and customs. Every religious preacher in India, during the past ages, worked in that line. Only the religion of Bhagavan Buddha was destructive. Hence that religion has been extirpated from India.

The disciple remembers that while thus speaking on, he remarked, "If the Brahman is manifested in one man, thousands of men advance, finding their way out in that light. Only the knowers of Brahman are the spiritual teachers of mankind. This is corroborated by all scriptures and by reason too. It is only the selfish Brahmins who have introduced into this country the system of hereditary Gurus, which is against the Vedas and against the

Shastras. Hence it is that even through their spiritual practice men do not now succeed in perfecting themselves or in realising Brahman. To remove all this corruption in religion, the Lord has incarnated Himself on earth in the present age in the person of Shri Ramakrishna. The universal teachings that he offered, if spread all over the world, will do good to humanity and the world. Not for many a century past has India produced so great, so wonderful, a teacher of religious synthesis."

A brother-disciple of Swamiji at that time asked him, "Why did you not publicly preach Shri Ramakrishna as an Avatâra in the West?"

Swamiji: They make much flourish and fuss over their science and philosophy. Hence, unless you first knock to pieces their intellectual conceit through reasoning, scientific argument, and philosophy, you cannot build anything there. Those who finding themselves off their moorings through their utmost intellectual reasoning would approach me in a real spirit of truth-seeking, to them alone, I would speak of Shri Ramakrishna. If, otherwise, I had forthwith spoken of the doctrine of incarnation, they might have said, "Oh, you do not say anything new — why, we have our Lord Jesus for all that!"

After thus spending some three or four delightful hours, the disciple came back to Calcutta that day along with the other visitors.

IV

(Translated from Bengali)

(From the Diary of a Disciple)

(The disciple is Sharatchandra Chakravarty, who published
his records in a Bengali book, *Swami-Shishya-Samvâda*, in two
parts. The present series of "Conversations and Dialogues" is a
revised translation from this book. Five dialogues of this series
have already appeared in the *Complete Works*, Vol. V.)

[Place: The Kali-temple at Dakshineswar and the Alambazar Math. Year: 1897, March.]

When Swamiji returned from England for the first time, the Ramakrishna Math was located at Alambazar. The birthday anniversary of Bhagavan Shri Ramakrishna was being celebrated this year at the Kali-temple of Rani Râsmani at Dakshineswar. Swamiji with some of his brother-disciples reached there from the Alambazar Math at about 9 or 10 a.m. He was barefooted, with a yellow turban on his head. Crowds of people were waiting to see and hear him. In the temple of Mother Kali, Swamiji prostrated himself before the Mother of the Universe, and thousands of heads, following him, bent low. Then after prostrating himself before Râdhâkântaji he came into the room which Shri Ramakrishna used to occupy. There was not the least breathing space in the room.

Two European ladies who accompanied Swamiji to India attended the festival. Swamiji took them along with himself to show them the holy Panchavati and the Vilva tree. Though the disciple was not yet quite familiar with Swamiji, he followed him, and presented him with the copy of a Sanskrit Ode about the Utsava (celebration) composed by himself. Swamiji read it while walking towards the Panchavati. And on the way he once looked aside towards the disciple and said, "Yes, it's done well. Attempt others like it."

The householder devotees of Shri Ramakrishna happened to be assembled on one side of the Panchavati, among whom was Babu Girish Chandra Ghosh. Swamiji, accompanied by a throng, came to Girish Babu and saluted him, saying, "Hello! here is Mr. Ghosh." Girish Babu returned his salutation with folded hands. Reminding Girish Babu of the old days, Swamiji said, "Think of it, Mr. Ghosh — from those days to these, what a transition! " Girish Babu endorsed Swamiji's sentiment and said, "Yes, that is true; but yet the mind longs to see more of it." After a short conversation, Swamiji proceeded towards the Vilva tree situated on the north-east of the Panchavati.

Now a huge crowd stood in keen expectancy to hear a lecture from Swamiji. But though he tried his utmost, Swamiji could not speak louder than the noise and clamour of the people. Hence he had to give up attempting a lecture and left with the two European ladies to show them sites connected with Shri Ramakrishna's spiritual practices and introduce them to particular devotees and followers of the Master.

After 3 p.m. Swamiji said to the disciple, "Fetch me a cab, please; I must go to the Math now." The disciple brought one accordingly. Swamiji himself sat on one side and asked Swami Niranjanananda and the disciple to sit on the other and they drove towards the Alambazar Math. On the way, Swamiji said to the disciple, "It won't do to live on abstract ideas merely. These festivals and the like are also necessary; for then only, these ideas will spread gradually among the masses. You see, the Hindus have got their festivals throughout the year, and the secret of it is to infuse the great ideals of religion gradually into the minds of the people. It has also its drawback, though. For people in general miss their inner significance and become so much engrossed in externals that no sooner are these festivities over than they become their old selves again. Hence it is true that all these form the outer covering of religion, which in a way hide real spirituality and self-knowledge.

"But there are those who cannot at all understand in the abstract what 'religion' is or what the 'Self' is, and they try to realise spirituality gradually through these festivals and ceremonies. Just take this festival celebrated today; those that attended it will at least once think of Shri Ramakrishna. The thought will occur to their mind as to who he was, in whose name such a great crowd assembled and why so many people came at all in his name. And those who will not feel that much even, will come once in a year to see all the devotional dancing and singing, or at least to partake of the sacred food-offerings, and will also have a look at the devotees of Shri Ramakrishna. This will rather benefit them than do any harm."

Disciple: But, sir, suppose somebody thinks these festivals and ceremonies to be the only thing essential, can he possibly advance any further? They will gradually come down to the level of commonplace observances, like the worship in our country of (the goddesses) Shashthi, Mangala-chandi, and the like. People are found to observe these rites till death; but where do we find even one among them rising through such observances to the knowledge of Brahman?

Swamiji: Why? In India so many spiritual heroes were born, and did they not make them the means of scaling the heights of greatness? When by persevering in practice through these props they gained a vision of the Self, they ceased to be keen on them. Yet, for the preservation of social balance even great men of the type of Incarnations follow these observances.

Disciple: Yes, they may observe these for appearance only. But when to a knower of the Self even this world itself becomes unreal like magic, is it possible for him to recognise these external observances as true?

Swamiji: Why not? Is not our idea of truth also a relative one, varying in relation to time, place, and person? Hence all observances have their utility, relatively to the varying qualifications in men. It is just as Shri Ramakrishna used to say, that the mother cooks Polâo and Kâlia (rich dishes) for one son, and sago for another.

Now the disciple understood at last and kept quiet. Meanwhile the carriage arrived at the Alambazar Math. The disciple followed Swamiji into the Math where Swamiji, being thirsty, drank some water. Then putting off his coat, he rested recumbent on the blanket spread on the floor. Swami Niranjanananda, seated by his side, said, "We never had such a great crowd in any year's Utsava before! As if the whole of Calcutta flocked there!"

Swamiji: It was quite natural; stranger things will happen hereafter.

Disciple: Sir, in every religious sect are found to exist external festivals of some kind or other. But there is no amity between one sect and another in this matter. Even in the case of such a liberal religion as that of Mohammed, I have found in Dacca that the Shiâs and Sunnis go to loggerheads with each other.

Swamiji: That is incidental more or less wherever you have sects. But do you know what the ruling sentiment amongst us is? — non-sectarianism. Our Lord was born to point that out. He would accept all forms, but would say withal that, looked at from the standpoint of the knowledge of Brahman, they were only like illusory Mâyâ.

Disciple: Sir, I can't understand your point. Sometimes it seems to me that, by thus celebrating these festivals, you are also inaugurating another sect round the name of Shri Ramakrishna. I have heard it from the lips of Nâg Mahâshaya that Shri Ramakrishna did not belong to any sect. He used to pay great respect to all creeds such as the Shâktas, the Vaishnavas, the Brahmos, the Mohammedans, and the Christians.

Swamiji: How do you know that we do not also hold in great esteem all the religious creeds?

So saying, Swamiji called out in evident amusement to Swami Niranjanananda: "Just think what this Bângâl is saying!"

Disciple: Kindly make me understand, sir, what you mean.

Swamiji: Well, you have, to be sure, read my lectures. But where have I built on Shri Ramakrishna's name? It is only the pure Upanishadic religion that I have gone about preaching in the world.

Disciple: That's true, indeed. But what I find by being familiar with you is that you have surrendered yourself, body and soul, to Ramakrishna. If you have understood Shri Ramakrishna to be the Lord Himself, why not give it out to the people at large?

Swamiji: Well, I do preach what I have understood. And if you have found the Advaitic principles of Vedanta to be the truest religion, then why don't you go out and preach it to all men?

Disciple: But I must realise, before I can preach it to others. I have only studied Advaitism in books.

Swamiji: Good; realise first and then preach. Now, therefore, you have no right to say anything of the beliefs each man tries to live by. For you also proceed now by merely putting your faith on some such beliefs.

Disciple: True, I am also living now by believing in something; but I have the Shâstras for my authority. I do not accept any faith opposed to the Shastras.

Swamiji: What do you mean by the Shastras? If the Upanishads are authority, why not the Bible or the Zend-Avesta equally so?

Disciple: Granted these scriptures are also good authority, they are not, however, as old as the Vedas. And nowhere, moreover, is the theory of the Âtman better established than in the Vedas.

Swamiji: Supposing I admit that contention of yours, what right have you to maintain that truth can be found nowhere except in the Vedas?

Disciple: Yes, truth may also exist in all the scriptures other than the Vedas, and I don't say anything to the contrary. But as for me, I choose to abide by the teachings of the Upanishads, for I have very great faith in them.

Swamiji: Quite welcome to do that, but if somebody else has "very great" faith in any other set of doctrines, surely you should allow him to abide by that. You will discover that in the long run both he and yourself will arrive at the same goal. For haven't you read in the *Mahimnah-stotram*, " त्वमसि पयसामर्णव इव — Thou art as the ocean to the rivers falling into it"?

V

(Translated from Bengali)
(From the Diary of a Disciple)

(The disciple is Sharatchandra Chakravarty, who published his records in a Bengali book, *Swami-Shishya-Samvâda*, in two parts. The present series of "Conversations and Dialogues" is a revised translation from this book. Five dialogues of this series have already appeared in the *Complete Works*, Vol. V.)

[Place: Alambazar Math. Year: 1897, May.]

It was the 19th Vaishâkha (April-May) of the year 1303 B.S. Swamiji had agreed to initiate the disciple today. So, early in the morning, he reached the Alambazar Math. Seeing the disciple Swamiji jocosely said, "Well, you are to be 'sacrificed' today, are you not?"

After this remark to the disciple, Swamiji with a smile resumed his talk with others about American subjects. And in due relevancy came along such topics also as how one-pointed in devotion one has to be in order to build up a spiritual life, how firm faith and strong devotion to the Guru have to be kept up, how deep reliance has to be placed on the words of the Guru, and how even one's life has to be laid down for his sake. Then putting some questions to the disciple, Swamiji began to test his heart: "Well, are you ready to do my bidding to your utmost, whatever it be and whenever it may come? If I ask you to plunge into the Ganga or to jump from the roof of a house, meaning it all for your good, could you do even that without any hesitation? Just think of it even now; otherwise don't rush forward on the spur of the moment to accept me as your Guru." And the disciple nodded assent to all questions of the kind.

Swamiji then continued: "The real Guru is he who leads you beyond this Mâyâ of endless birth and death — who graciously destroys all the griefs and maladies of the soul. The disciple of old used to repair to the hermitage of the Guru, fuel in hand; and the Guru, after ascertaining his competence, would teach him the Vedas after initiation, fastening round his waist the threefold filament of Munja, a kind of grass, as the emblem of his vow to keep his body, mind, and speech in control. With the help of this girdle, the disciples used to tie up their Kaupinas. Later on, the custom of wearing the sacred thread superseded this girdle of Munja grass."

Disciple: Would you, then, say, sir, that the use of the holy thread we have adopted is not really a Vedic custom?

Swamiji: Nowhere is there mention of thread being so used in the Vedas. The modern author of Smritis, Raghunandana Bhattacharya, also puts it thus: "At this stage, the sacrificial girdle should be put on." Neither in Gobhila's *Grihya-Sutras* do we find any mention of the girdle made of thread. In the Shâstras, this first Vedic Samskâra (purification ceremony) before the Guru has been called the Upanayana; but see, to what a sad pass our country has been brought! Straying away from the true path of the Shastras, the country has been overwhelmed with usages and observances originating in particular localities, or popular opinion, or with the womenfolk! That's why I ask you to proceed along the path of the Shastras as in olden times. Have faith within yourselves and thereby bring it back into the country. Plant in your heart the faith of Nachiketâ. Even go up to the world of Yama like him. Yes, if to know the secrets of the Atman, to liberate your soul, to reach the true solution of the mystery of birth and death, you have to go to the very jaws of death and realise the truth thereby, well, go there with an undaunted heart. It is fear alone that is death. You have to go beyond all fear. So from this day be fearless. Off at once, to lay down your life for your own liberation and for the good of others. What good is it carrying along a load of bones and flesh! Initiated into the Mantra of extreme self-sacrifice for the sake of God, go, lay down for others this body of flesh and bones like the Muni Dadhichi! Those alone, say the Shastras, are the real Gurus, who have studied the Vedas and the Vedanta, who are knowers of the Brahman, who are able to lead others beyond to fearlessness; when such are at hand, get yourself initiated, "no speculation in such a case". Do you know what has become of this principle now? — "like the blind leading the blind"!

* * *

The initiation ceremony was duly gone through in the chapel. After this Swamiji spoke out: "Give me the Guru-dakshinâ." The disciple replied, "Oh, what shall I give?" On this Swamiji suggested, "Well, fetch any fruit from the store-room." So the disciple ran to the store-room and came back into the chapel with ten or twelve lichis. These Swamiji took from his hand and ate them one by one, saying, "Now, your Guru-dakshina is made."

A member of the Math, Brahmachâri (now Swami) Shuddhananda, also had his initiation from Swamiji on this occasion.

Swamiji then had his dinner and went to take a short rest.

After the siesta, he came and sat in the hall of the upper storey. The disciple finding this opportunity asked, "Sir, how and whence came the ideas of virtue and vice?"

Swamiji: It is from the idea of the manifold that these have evolved. The more a man advances towards oneness, the more ideas of "I" and "you" subside, ideas from which all these pairs of opposites such as virtue and vice have originated. When the idea that So-and-so is different from me comes to the mind, all other ideas of distinction begin to manifest, while with the complete realisation of oneness, no more grief or illusion remains for man, " तत्र को मोहः कः शोकः एकत्वमनुपश्यतः — For him who sees oneness, where is there any grief or any delusion?" Sin may be said to be the feeling of every kind of weakness. From this weakness spring jealousy, malice, and so forth. Hence weakness is sin. The Self within is always shining forth resplendent. Turning away from that people say "I", "I", "I", with their attention held up by this material body, this queer cage of flesh and bones. This is the root of all weakness. From that habit only, the relative outlook on life has emerged in this world. The absolute Truth lies beyond that duality.

Disciple: Well, is then all this relative experience not true?

Swamiji: As long as the idea of "I" remains, it is true. And the instant the realisation of "I" as the Atman comes, this world of relative existence becomes false. What people speak of as sin is the result of weakness — is but another form of the egoistic idea, "I am the body". When the mind gets steadfast in the truth, "I am the Self", then you go beyond merit and demerit, virtue and vice. Shri Ramakrishna used to say, "When the 'I' dies, all trouble is at an end."

Disciple: Sir, this "I" has a most tenacious life. It is very difficult to kill it.

Swamiji: Yes, in one sense, it is very difficult, but in another sense, it is quite easy. Can you tell me where this "I" exists? How can you speak of anything being killed, which never exists at all? Man only remains hypnotised with the false idea of an ego. When this ghost is off from us, all dreams vanish, and then it is found that the one Self only exists from the highest Being to a blade of grass. This will have to be known, to be realised. All practice or worship is only for taking off this veil. When that will go, you will find that the Sun of Absolute Knowledge is shining in Its own lustre. For the Atman only is self-luminous and has to be realised by Itself. How can that, which can be experienced only by itself be known with the help of any other thing? Hence the Shruti says, तत्र को मोहः कः शोकः एकत्वमनुपश्यतः " — Well, through what means is that to be known which is the Knower?" Whatever you know, you know through the instrumentality of your mind.

But mind is something material. It is active only because there is the pure Self behind it. So, how can you know that Self through your mind? But this only becomes known, after all, that the mind cannot reach the pure Self, no, nor even the intellect. Our relative knowledge ends just there. Then, when the mind is free from activity or functioning, it vanishes, and the Self is revealed. This state has been described by the commentator Shankara as अपरोक्षानुभूतिः or supersensuous perception.

Disciple: But, sir, the mind itself is the "I". If that mind is gone, then the "I" also cannot remain.

Swamiji: Yes, the state that comes then is the real nature of the ego. The "I" that remains then is omnipresent, all-pervading, the Self of all. Just as the Ghatâkâsha, when the jar is broken, becomes the Mahâkâsha, for with the destruction of the jar the enclosed space is not destroyed. The puny "I" which you were thinking of as confined in the body, becomes spread out and is thus realised in the form of the all-pervading "I" or the Self. Hence what matters it to the real "I" or the Self, whether the mind remains or is destroyed? What I say you will realise in course of time. "कालेनात्मनि विन्दति — It is realised within oneself in due time." As you go on with Shravana and Manana (proper hearing and proper thinking), you will fully understand it in due time and then you will go beyond mind. Then there will be no room for any such question.

Hearing all this, the disciple remained quiet on his seat, and Swamiji, as he gently smoked, continued: "How many Shastras have been written to explain this simple thing, and yet men fail to understand it! How they are vesting this precious human life on the fleeting pleasures of some silver coins and the frail beauty of women! Wonderful is the influence of Mahâmâyâ (Divine Illusion)! Mother! Oh Mother!"

VI

(Translated from Bengali)
(From the Diary of a Disciple)

(The disciple is Sharatchandra Chakravarty, who published his records in a Bengali book, *Swami-Shishya-Samvâda*, in two parts. The present series of "Conversations and Dialogues" is a revised translation from this book. Five dialogues of this series have already appeared in the *Complete Works*, Vol. V.)

[Place: Baghbazar, Calcutta. Year: 1897.]

Swamiji has been staying for some days at the house of the late Balaram Babu. At his wish, a large number of devotees of Shri Ramakrishna have assembled at the house at 3 p.m. (on May 1, 1897). Swami Yogananda is amongst those present here. The object of Swamiji is to form an Association. When all present had taken their seats, Swamiji proceeded to speak as follows:

"The conviction has grown in my mind after all my travels in various lands that no great cause can succeed without an organisation. In a country like ours, however, it does not seem quite practicable to me to start an organisation at once with a democratic basis or work by general voting. People in the West are more educated in this respect, and less jealous of one another than ourselves. They have learnt to respect merit. Take for instance my case. I was just an insignificant man there, and yet see how cordially they received and entertained me. When with the spread of education the masses in our country grow more sympathetic and liberal, when they learn to have their thoughts expanded beyond the limits of sect or party, then it will be possible to work; on the democratic basis of organization. For this reason it is necessary to have a dictator for this Society. Everybody should obey him, and then in time we may work on the principle of general voting.

"Let this Association be named after him, in whose name indeed, we have embraced the monastic life, with whom as your Ideal in life you all toil on the field of work from your station in family life, within twenty years of whose passing away a wonderful diffusion of his holy name and extraordinary life has taken place both in the East and the West. We are the servants of the Lord. Be you all helpers in this cause."

When Srijut Girish Chandra Ghosh and all other householder disciples present had approved of the above proposal, the future programme of the Society of Shri Ramakrishna was taken up for discussion. The Society was named the Ramakrishna Mission.

Swamiji himself became the general president of the Mission and other office-bearers also were elected. The rule was laid down that the Association should hold meetings at the house of Balaram Babu every Sunday at 4 p.m. Needless to say that Swamiji used to attend these meetings whenever convenient.

When the meeting had broken up and the members departed, addressing Swami Yogananda, Swamiji said, "So the work is now begun this way; let us see how far it succeeds by the will of Shri Ramakrishna."

Swami Yogananda: You are doing these things with Western methods. Should you say Shri Ramakrishna left us any such instructions?

Swamiji: Well, how do you know that all this is not on Shri Ramakrishna's lines? He had an infinite breadth of feeling, and dare you shut him up within your own limited views of life. I will break down these limits and scatter broadcast over the earth his boundless inspiration. He never instructed me to introduce any rites of his own worship. We have to realise the teachings he has left us about religious practice and devotion, concentration and meditation, and such higher ideas and truths, and then preach these to all men. The infinite number of faiths are only so many paths. I haven't been born to found one more sect in a world already teeming with sects. We have been blessed with obtaining refuge at the feet of the Master, and we are born to carry his message to the dwellers of the three worlds.

Swami Yogananda uttered no word of dissent, and so Swamiji continued: Time and again have I received in this life marks of his grace. He stands behind and gets all this work done by me. When lying helpless under a tree in an agony of hunger, when I had not even a scrap of cloth for Kaupina, when I was resolved on travelling penniless round the world, even then help came in all ways by the grace of Shri Ramakrishna. And again when crowds jostled with one another in the streets of Chicago to have a sight of this Vivekananda, then also, just because I had his grace, I could digest without difficulty all that honour — a hundredth part of which would have been enough to turn mad any ordinary man; and by his will, victory followed everywhere. Now I must conclude by doing something in this country. So casting all doubt away, please help my work; and you will find everything fulfilled by his will.

Swami Yogananda: Yes, whatever you will, shall be fulfilled; and are we not all ever obedient to you? Now and then I do clearly see how

Shri Ramakrishna is getting all these things done through you. And yet, to speak plainly, some misgiving rises at intervals, for as we saw it, his was of doing things was different. So I question myself: "Are we sure that we are not going astray from Shri Ramakrishna's teachings?" And so I take the opposing attitude and warn you.

Swamiji: You see, the fact is that Shri Ramakrishna is not exactly what the ordinary followers have comprehended him to be. He had infinite moods and phases. Even if you might form an idea of the limits of Brahmajnâna, the knowledge of the Absolute, you could not have any idea of the unfathomable depths of his mind! Thousands of Vivekanandas may spring forth through one gracious glance of his eyes! But instead of doing that, he has chosen to get things done this time through me as his single instrument, and what can I do in this matter you see?

Saying this, Swamiji left to attend to something else waiting for him, and Swami Yogananda went on praising Swamiji's versatile gifts.

Meanwhile Swamiji returned and asked the disciple, "Do the people in your part of the country know much of Shri Ramakrishna?"

Disciple: Only one man, Nâg Mahâshaya, came to Shri Ramakrishna from our part of Bengal; it is from him that many came to hear of him and had their curiosity excited to know more. But that Shri Ramakrishna was the Incarnation of God, the people there have not yet come to know and some would not believe it even if told so.

Swamiji: Do you think it is an easy matter to believe so? We who had actual dealings with him in every respect we who heard of that fact again and again from his own lips, we who lived and stayed with him for twenty-four hours of the day — even we off and on have doubts about it coming over us! So what to speak of others!

Disciple: Did Shri Ramakrishna, out of his own lips ever say that he was God, the all-perfect Brahman?

Swamiji: Yes, he did so many times. And he said this to all of us. One day while was staying at the Cossipore garden, his body in imminent danger of falling off for ever, by the side of his bed I was saying in my mind, "Well, now if you can declare that you are God, then only will I believe you are really God Himself." It was only two days before he passed away. Immediately, he looked up towards me all on a sudden and said, "He who was Rama, He who was Krishna, verily is He now Ramakrishna in this body. And that not merely from the standpoint of your Vedanta!" At this I was struck dumb. Even we haven't had yet the perfect faith, after hearing it again and again from the holy lips of our Lord himself — our minds still get disturbed now and then with doubt and despair — and so, what shall we speak of others being slow to believe? It is indeed a very difficult matter to be able to declare and believe a man with a body like ours to be God Himself. We may just go to the length of declaring him to be a "perfected one", or a "knower of Brahman". Well, it matters nothing, whatever you may call him or think of him, a saint, or a knower of Brahman, or anything. But take it from me, never did come to this earth such an all-perfect man as Shri Ramakrishna! In the utter darkness of the world, this great man is like the shining pillar of illumination in this age! And by his light alone will man now cross the ocean of Samsâra!

Disciple: To me it seems, sir, that true faith comes only after actually seeing or hearing something. Mathur Babu, I have heard, actually saw so many things about Shri Ramakrishna, and thus he had that wonderful faith in him.

Swamiji: He who believes not, believes not even after seeing, and thinks that it is all hallucination, or dream and so on. The great transfiguration of Krishna — the Vishvarupa (form universal) — was seen alike by Duryodhana and by Arjuna. But only Arjuna believed, while Duryodhana took it to be magic! Unless He makes us understand, nothing can be stated or understood. Somebody comes to the fullest faith even without seeing or hearing, while somebody else remains plunged in doubt even after witnessing with his own eyes various extraordinary powers for twelve years! The secret of it all is His grace! But then one must persevere, so that the grace may be received.

Disciple: Is there, sir, any law of grace?

Swamiji: Yes and no.

Disciple: How is that?

Swamiji: Those who are pure always in body, mind, and speech, who have strong devotion, who discriminate between the real and the unreal, who persevere in meditation and contemplation — upon them alone the grace of the Lord descends. The Lord, however, is beyond all natural laws — is not under any rules and regulations, or just as Shri Ramakrishna used to say, He has the child's nature — and that's why we find some failing to get any response even after calling on Him for millions of births, while some one else whom we regard as a sinful or penitent man or a disbeliever, would have Illumination in a flash! — On the latter the Lord perhaps lavishes His grace quite unsolicited! You may argue that this man had good merits stored up from previous life, but the mystery is really difficult to understand. Shri Ramakrishna used to say sometimes, "Do rely on Him; be like the dry leaf at the mercy of the wind"; and again he would say, "The wind of His grace is always blowing, what you need to do is to unfurl your sail."

Disciple: But, sir, this is a most tremendous statement. No reasoning, I see, can stand here.

Swamiji: Ah, all reasoning and arguing is within the limit of the realm of Maya; it lies within the categories of space, time, and causation. But He is beyond these categories. We speak of His law, still He is beyond all law. He creates, or becomes, all that we speak of as laws of nature, and yet He is outside of them all. He on whom His grace descends, in a moment goes beyond all law. For this reason there is no condition in grace. It is as His play or sport. And this creation of the universe is like His play — "लोकवत् लीलाकैवल्यम् — It is the pure delight of sport, as in the case of men" (*Vedanta-Sutras*, II. i. 33). Is it not possible for Him who creates and destroys the universe as if in play to grant salvation by grace to the greatest sinner? But then it is just His pleasure, His play, to get somebody through the practice of spiritual discipline and somebody else without it.

Disciple: Sir, I can't understand this.

Swamiji: And you needn't. Only get your mind to cling to Him as far as you can. For then only the great magic of this world will break of itself. But then, you must persevere. You must take off your mind from lust and lucre, must discriminate always between the real and the unreal — must settle down into the mood of bodilessness with the brooding thought that you are not this body, and must always have the realisation that you are the all-pervading Atman. This persevering practice is called Purushakâra (self-exertion — as distinguished from grace). By such self-exertion will come true reliance on Him, and that is the goal of human achievement.

After a pause Swamiji resumed: Had you not been receiving His grace, why else would you come here at all? Shri Ramakrishna used to say, "Those who have had the grace of God cannot but come here. Wherever they might be, whatever they might be doing, they are sure to be affected by words or sentiments uttered from here." Just take your own case — do you think it is possible without the grace of God to have the blessed company of Nag Mahashaya, a man who rose to spiritual perfection through the strength of divine grace and came to know fully what this grace really means? "अनेकजन्मसंसिद्धस्ततो याति परां गतिम् — One attains the highest stage after being perfected by the practice of repeated births" (Gita, VI. 45). It is only by virtue of great religious merit acquired through many births that one comes across a great soul like him. All the characteristics of the highest type of Bhakti, spoken of in the scriptures, have manifested themselves in Nag Mahashaya. It is only in him that we actually see fulfilled the widely quoted text, " ". ("Lowlier than the lowly stalk of grass.") Blessed indeed is your East Bengal to have been hallowed by the touch of Nag Mahashaya's feet!

While speaking thus, Swamiji rose to pay a visit to the great poet, Babu Girish Chandra Ghosh. Swami Yogananda and the disciple followed him. Reaching Girish Babu's place, Swamiji seated himself and said, "You see, G. C., the impulse is constantly coming nowadays to my mind to do this and to do that, to scatter broadcast on earth the message of Shri Ramakrishna and so on. But I pause again to reflect, lest all this give rise to another sect in India. So I have to work with a good deal of caution. Sometimes I think, what if a sect does grow up. But then again the thought comes! 'No. Shri Ramakrishna never disturbed anybody's own spiritual outlook; he always looked at the inner sameness.' Often do I restrain myself with this thought. Now, what do you say?"

Girish Babu: What can I say to this? You are the instrument in his hand. You have to do just what he would have you do. I don't trouble myself over the detail. But I see that the power of the Lord is getting things done by you, I see it clear as daylight.

Swamiji: But I think we do things according to our own will. Yet, that in misfortunes and adversities, in times of want and poverty, he reveals himself to us and guides us along the true path — this I have been able to realise. But alas, I still fail to comprehend in any way the greatness of his power.

Girish Babu: Yes, he said, "If you understand it to the full, everything will at once vanish. Who will work then or who will be made to work?"

After this the talk drifted on to America. And Swamiji grew warm on his subject and went on describing the wonderful wealth of the country, the virtues and defects of men and women there, their luxury and so on.

VII

(Translated from Bengali)

(From the Diary of a Disciple)

(The disciple is Sharatchandra Chakravarty, who published his records in a Bengali book, *Swami-Shishya-Samvâda*, in two parts. The present series of "Conversations and Dialogues" is a revised translation from this book. Five dialogues of this series have already appeared in the *Complete Works*, Vol. V.)

[*Place: Calcutta.* Year: *1897.*]

For some days past, Swamiji has been staying at Balaram Bose's house, Baghbazar. There will be a total eclipse of the sun today. The disciple is to cook for Swamiji this morning, and on his presenting himself, Swamiji said, "Well, the cooking must be in the East Bengal style; and we must finish our dinner before the eclipse starts."

The inner apartments of the house were all unoccupied now. So the disciple went inside into the kitchen and started his cooking. Swamiji also was looking in now and then with a word of encouragement and sometimes with a joke, as, "Take care, the soup (The Bengali expression has a peculiar pronunciation in East Bengal which gives the point of the joke.) must be after the East Bengal fashion."

The cooking had been almost completed, when Swamiji came in after his bath and sat down for dinner, putting up his own seat and plate. "Do bring in anything finished, quick," he said, "I can't wait, I'm burning with hunger!" While eating, Swamiji was pleased with the curry with bitters and remarked, "Never have I enjoyed such a nice thing! But none of the things is so hot as your soup." "It's just after the style of the Burdwan District", said Swamiji tasting the sour preparation. He then brought his dinner to a close and after washing sat on the bedstead inside the room. While having his after-dinner smoke, Swamiji remarked to the disciple, "Whoever cannot cook well cannot become a good Sâdhu; unless the mind is pure, good tasteful cooking is not possible. "

Soon after this, the sound of bells and conch-shells, etc., rose from all quarters, when Swamiji said, "Now that the eclipse has begun, let me sleep, and you please massage my feet!" Gradually the eclipse covered the whole of the sun's disc and all around fell the darkness of dusk.

While there were fifteen or twenty minutes left for the eclipse to pass off, Swamiji rose from his siesta, and after washing, jocosely said while taking a smoke, "Well, people say that whatever one does during an eclipse, one gets that millionfold in future; so I thought that the Mother, Mahâmâyâ, did not ordain that this body might have good sleep, and if I could get some sleep during the eclipse, I might have plenty of it in future. But it all failed, for I slept only for fifteen minutes at the most."

After this, at the behest of Swamiji some short speeches were made. There was yet an hour left before dusk. When all had assembled in the parlour, Swamiji told them to put him any question they liked.

Swami Shuddhananda asked, "What is the real nature of meditation, sir?"

Swamiji: Meditation is the focusing of the mind on some object. If the mind acquires concentration on one object, it can be so concentrated on any object whatsoever.

Disciple: Mention is made in the scriptures of two kinds of meditation — one having some object and the other objectless. What is meant by all that, and which of the two is the higher one?

Swamiji: First, the practice of meditation has to proceed with some one object before the mind. Once I used to concentrate my mind on some black point. Ultimately, during those days, I could not see the point any more, nor notice that the point was before me at all — the mind used to be no more — no wave of functioning would rise, as if it were all an ocean without any breath of air. In that state I used to experience glimpses of supersensuous truth. So I think, the practice of meditation even with some trifling external object leads to mental concentration. But it is true that the mind very easily attains calmness when one practices meditation with anything on which one's mind is most apt to settle down. This is the reason why we have in this country so much worship of the images of gods and goddesses. And what wonderful art developed from such worship! But no more of that now. The fact, however, is that the objects of meditation can never be the same in the case of all men. People have proclaimed and preached to others only those external objects to which they held on to become perfected in meditation. Oblivious of the fact, later on, that these objects are aids to the attainment of perfect mental calmness, men have extolled them beyond everything else. They have wholly concerned themselves with the means, getting comparatively unmindful of the end. The real aim is to make the mind functionless, but this cannot be got at unless one becomes absorbed in some object.

Disciple: But if the mind becomes completely engrossed and identified with some object, how can it give us the consciousness of Brahman?

Swamiji: Yes, though the mind at first assumes the form of the object, yet later on the consciousness of that object vanishes. Then only the experience of pure "isness" remains.

Disciple: Well, sir, how is it that desires rise even after mental concentration is acquired?

Swamiji: Those are the outcome of previous Samskâras (deep-rooted impressions or tendencies). When Buddha was on the point of merging in Samadhi (superconsciousness), Mâra made his appearance. There was really no Mara extraneous to the mind; it was only the external reflection of the mind's previous Samskaras.

Disciple: But one hears of various fearful experiences prior to the attainment of perfection. Are they all mental projections?

Swamiji: What else but that? The aspiring soul, of course, does not make out at that time that all these are external manifestations of his own mind. But all the same, there is nothing outside of it. Even what you see as this world does not exist outside. It is all a mental projection. When the mind becomes functionless, it reflects the Brahman-consciousness. Then the vision of all spheres of existence may supervene, "यं यं लोकं मनसा संविभाति — Whatsoever sphere one may call up in mind" (Mundaka, III. i. 10). Whatsoever is resolved on becomes realised at once. He who, even on attaining this state of unfalsified self-determination, preserves his watchfulness and is free from the bondage of desire, verily attains to the knowledge of Brahman. But he who loses his balance after reaching this state gets the manifold powers, but falls off from the Supreme goal.

So saying, Swamiji began to repeat "Shiva, Shiva", and then continued: There is no way, none whatsoever, to the solution of the profound mystery of this life except through renunciation. Renunciation, renunciation and renunciation — let this be the one motto of your lives. "सर्वं वस्तु भयान्वितं भुवि नृणां वैराग्यमेवाभयम् — For men, all things on earth are infected with fear, Vairâgya (renunciation) alone constitutes fearlessness" (*Vairâgya-Shatakam*).

VIII

(Translated from Bengali)
(From the Diary of a Disciple)

(The disciple is Sharatchandra Chakravarty, who published his records in a Bengali book, *Swami-Shishya-Samvâda*, in two parts. The present series of "Conversations and Dialogues" is a revised translation from this book. Five dialogues of this series have already appeared in the *Complete Works*, Vol. V.)

[*Place: Calcutta. Year: 1897, March or April.*]

Today the disciple came to meet Swamiji at Baghbazar, but found him ready for a visiting engagement. "Well, come along with me", were the words with which Swamiji accosted him as he went downstairs, and the disciple followed. They then put themselves into a hired cab which proceeded southwards.

Disciple: Sir, where are you going to visit, please?

Swamiji: Well, come with me and you will see.

Thus keeping back the destination from the disciple, Swamiji opened the following conversation as the carriage reached the Beadon Street: One does not find any real endeavour in your country to get the women educated. You, the men are educating yourselves to develop your manhood, but what are you doing to educate and advance those who share all your happiness and misery, who lay down their lives to serve you in your homes?

Disciple: Why, sir, just see how many schools and colleges hare sprung up nowadays for our women, and how many of them are getting degrees of B.A. and M.A.

Swamiji: But all that is in the Western style. How many schools have been started on your own national lines, in the spirit of your own religious ordinances? But alas, such a system does not obtain even among the men of your country, what to speak of women! It is seen from the official statistics that only three or four per cent of the people in India are educated, and not even one per cent of the women.

Otherwise, how could the country come to such a fallen condition? How can there be any progress of the country without the spread of education, the dawning of knowledge? Even no real effort or exertion in the cause is visible among the few in your country who are the promise of the future, you who have received the blessings of education. But know for certain that absolutely nothing can be done to improve the state of things, unless there is spread of education first among the women and the masses. And so I have it in my mind to train up some Brahmachârins and Brahmachârinis, the former of whom will eventually take the vow of Sannyâsa and try to carry the light of education among the masses, from village to village, throughout the country, while the latter will do the same among women. But the whole work must be done in the style of our own country. Just as centres have to be started for men, so also centres have to be started for teaching women. Brahmacharinis of education and character should take up the task of teaching at these different centres. History and the Purânas, housekeeping and the arts, the duties of home-life and principles that make for the development of an ideal character have to be taught with the help of modern science, and the women students must be trained up in ethical and spiritual life. We must see to their growing up as ideal matrons of home in time. The children of such mothers will make further progress in the virtues that distinguish the mothers. It is only in the homes of educated and pious mothers that great men are born. And you have reduced your women to something like manufacturing machines; alas, for heaven's sake, is this the outcome of your education? The uplift of the women, the awakening of the masses must come first, and then only can any real good come about for the country, for India.

Near Chorebagan Swamiji gave it out to the disciple that the foundress of the Mahâkali Pâthashâlâ, the Tapasvini Mâtâji (ascetic mother), had invited him to visit her institution. When our carriage stopped at its destination, three or four gentlemen greeted Swamiji and showed him up to the first door. There the Tapasvini mother received him standing. Presently she escorted him into one of the classes, where all the maidens stood up in greeting. At a word from Mataji all of them commenced reciting the Sanskrit meditation of Lord Shiva with proper intonation. Then they demonstrated at the instance of the Mother how they were taught the ceremonies of worship in their school. After watching all this with much delight and interest, Swamiji proceeded to visit the other classes. After this, Mataji sent for some particular girl and asked her to explain before Swamiji the first verse of the third canto of Kalidasa's *Raghavamsham*, which she did in Sanskrit. Swamiji expressed his great appreciation of the measure of success Mataji had attained by her perseverance and application in the cause of diffusing education among women. In reply, she said with much humility, "In my service to my students, I look upon them as the Divine Mother; well, in starting the school I have neither fame nor any other object in view."

Being asked by Mataji, Swamiji recorded his opinion about the institution in the Visitors' Book, the last line of which was: "The movement is in the right direction."

After saluting Mataji, Swamiji went back to his carriage, which then proceeded towards Baghbazar, while the following conversation took place between Swamiji and the disciple.

Swamiji: How far is the birthplace of this venerable lady! She has renounced everything of her worldly life, and yet how diligent in the service of humanity! Had she not been a woman, could she ever have undertaken the teaching of women in the way she is doing? What I saw here was all good, but that some male householders should be pitchforked as teachers is a thing I cannot approve of. The duty of teaching in the school ought to devolve in every respect on educated widows and Brahmacharinis. It is good to avoid in this country any association of men with women's schools.

Disciple: But, sir, how would you get now in thin country learned and virtuous women like Gârgi, Khanâ or Lilâvati?

Swamiji: Do you think women of the type don't exist now in the country? Still on this sacred soil of India, this land of Sitâ and Sâvitri, among women may be found such character, such spirit of service, such affection, compassion, contentment, and reverence, as I could not find anywhere else in the world! In the West, the women did not very often seem to me to be women at all, they appeared to be quite the replicas of men! Driving vehicles, drudging in offices, attending schools, doing professional duties! In India alone the sight of feminine modesty and reserve soothes the eye! With such materials of great promise, you could not, alas, work out their uplift! You did not try to infuse the light of knowledge into them. If they get the right sort of education, they may well turn out to be the ideal women in the world.

Disciple: Do you think, sir, the same consummation would be reached through the way Mataji is educating her students? These students would soon grow up and get married and would presently shade into the likeness of all other women of the common run. So I think, if these girls might be made to adopt Brahmacharya, then only could they devote their lives to the cause of the country's progress and attain to the high ideals preached in our sacred books.

Swamiji: Yes, everything will come about in time. Such educated men are not yet born in this country, who can keep their girls unmarried without fear of social punishment. Just see how before the girls exceed the age of twelve or thirteen, people hasten to give them away in marriage out of this fear of their social equals. Only the other day, when the Age of Consent Bill was being passed, the leaders of society massed together millions of men to send up the cry "We don't want the Bill." Had this been in any other country, far from getting up meetings to send forth a cry like that, people would have hidden their heads under their roofs in shame, that such a calumny could yet stain their society.

Disciple: But, sir, I don't think the ancient law-givers supported this custom of early marriage without any rhyme or reason. There must have been some secret meaning in this attitude of theirs.

Swamiji: Well, what might have been this secret meaning, please?

Disciple: Take it, for instance, in the first place that if the girls are married at an early age, they may come over to their husbands' home to learn the particular ways and usages of the family from the early years of their life. They may acquire adequate skill in the duties of the household under the guidance of their parents-in-law. In the homes of their own parents, on the other hand, there is the likelihood of grown-up daughters going astray. But married early, they have no chance of thus going wrong, and over and above this, such feminine virtues as modesty, reserve, fortitude, and diligence are apt to develop in them.

Swamiji: In favour of the other side of the question, again, it may be argued that early marriage leads to premature child-bearing, which accounts for most of our women dying early; their progeny also, being of low vitality, go to swell the ranks of our country's beggars! For if the physique of the parents be not strong and healthy, how can strong and healthy children be born at all? Married a little later and bred in culture, our mothers will give birth to children who would be able to achieve the real good of the country. The reason why you have so many widows in every home lies here, in this custom of early marriage. If the number of early marriages declines, that of widows is bound to follow suit.

Disciple: But, sir, it seems to me, if our women are married late in life, they are apt to be less mindful of their household duties. I have heard that the mothers-in-law in Calcutta very often do all the cooking, while the educated daughters-in-law sit idle with red paint round their feet! But in our East Bengal such a thing is never allowed to take place.

Swamiji: But everywhere under the sun you find the same blending of the good and the bad. In my opinion society in every country shapes itself out of its own initiative. So we need not trouble our heads prematurely about such reforms as the abolition of early marriage, the remarriage of widows, and so on. Our part of the duty lies in imparting true education to all men and women in society. As an outcome of that education, they will of themselves be able to know what is good for them and what is bad, and will spontaneously eschew the latter. It will not be then necessary to pull down or set up anything in society by coercion.

Disciple: What sort of education, do you think, is suited to our women?

Swamiji: Religion, arts, science, housekeeping, cooking, sewing, hygiene — the simple essential points in these subjects ought to be taught to our women. It is not good to let them touch novels and fiction. The Mahakali Pathashala is to a great extent moving in the right direction. But only teaching rites of worship won't do; their education must be an eye-opener in all matters. Ideal characters must always be presented before the view of the girls to imbue them with a devotion to lofty principles of selflessness. The noble examples of Sita, Savitri, Damavanti, Lilavati, Khana, and Mirâ should be brought home to their minds and they should be inspired to mould their own lives in the light of these.

Our cab now reached the house of the late Babu Balaram Bose at Baghbazar. Swamiji alighted from it and went upstairs. There he recounted the whole of his experience at the Mahakali Pathashala to those who had assembled there to see him.

Then while discussing what the members of the newly formed Ramakrishna Mission should do, Swamiji proceeded to establish by various arguments the supreme importance of the "gift of learning" and the "gift of knowledge". (The allusion here is to the classification of various gifts, mentioned by Manu.) Turning to the disciple he said, "Educate, educate, ' " नान्यः पन्था विद्यतेऽयनाय ' — Than this there is no other way'." And referring in banter to the party who do not favour educational propaganda, he said, "Well, don't go into the party of Prahlâdas!" Asked as to the meaning of the expression he replied, "Oh, haven't you heard? Tears rushed out of the eyes of Prahlada at the very sight of the first letter 'Ka' of the alphabet as it reminded him of Krishna; so how could any studies be proceeded with? But then the tears in Prahlada's eyes were tears of love, while your fools affect tears in fright! Many of the devotees are also like that." All of those present burst out laughing on hearing this, and Swami Yogananda said to Swamiji, "Well, once you have the urge within towards anything to be done, you won't have any peace until you see the utmost done about it. Now what you have a mind to have done shall be done no doubt."

IX

(Translated from Bengali)

(From the Diary of a Disciple)

(The disciple is Sharatchandra Chakravarty, who published
his records in a Bengali book, *Swami-Shishya-Samvâda*, in two
parts. The present series of "Conversations and Dialogues" is a
revised translation from this book. Five dialogues of this series
have already appeared in the *Complete Works*, Vol. V.)

[Place: Calcutta. year: 1897.]

For the last ten days, the disciple had been studying Sâyana's commentary on the Rig-Veda with Swamiji, who was staying then at the house of the late Babu Balaram Bose at Baghbazar. Max Müller's volumes on the Rig-Veda had been brought from a wealthy friend's private library. Swamiji was correcting the disciple every now and then and giving him the true pronunciation or construction as necessary. Sometimes while explaining the arguments of Sayana to establish the eternity of the Vedas, Swamiji was praising very highly the commentator's wonderful ingenuity; sometimes again while arguing out the deeper significance of the doctrine, he was putting forward a difference in view and indulging in an innocent squib at Sayana.

While our study had proceeded thus for a while, Swamiji raised the topic about Max Müller and continued thus: Well, do you know, my impression is that it is Sayana who is born again as Max Müller to revive his own commentary on the Vedas? I have had this notion for long. It became confirmed in my mind, it seems, after I had seen Max Müller. Even here in this country, you don't find a scholar so persevering, and so firmly grounded in the Vedas and the Vedanta. Over and above this, what a deep, unfathomable respect for Shri Ramakrishna! Do you know, he believes in his Divine Incarnation! And what great hospitality towards me when I was his guest! Seeing the old man and his lady, it seemed to me that they were living their home-life like another Vasishtha and Arundhati! At the time of parting with me, tears came into the eyes of the old man.

Disciple: But, sir, if Sayana himself became Max Müller, then why was he born as a Mlechchha instead of being born in the sacred land of India?

Swamiji: The feeling and the distinction that I am an Aryan and the other is a Mlechchha come from ignorance. But what are Varnâshrama and caste divisions to one who is the commentator of the Vedas, the shining embodiment of knowledge? To him they are wholly meaningless, and he can assume human birth wherever he likes for doing good to mankind. Specially, if he did not choose to be born in a land which excelled both in learning and wealth, where would he secure the large expenses for publishing such stupendous volumes? Didn't you hear that the East India Company paid nine lakhs of rupees in cash to have the Rig-Veda published? Even this money was not enough. Hundreds of Vedic Pundits had to be employed in this country on monthly stipends. Has anybody seen in this age, here in this country, such profound yearning for knowledge, such prodigious investment of money for the sake of light and learning? Max Müller himself has written it in his preface, that for twenty-five years he prepared only the manuscripts. Then the printing took another twenty years! It is not possible for an ordinary man to drudge for fortyfive years of his life with one publication. Just think of it! Is it an idle fancy of mine to say he is Sayana himself?

After this talk about Max Müller the leading of the Vedas was resumed. Now Swamiji began variously to support the view of Sayana that creation proceeded out of the Vedas. He said: Veda means the sum total of eternal truths; the Vedic Rishis experienced those truths; they can be experienced only by seers of the supersensuous and not by common men like us. That is why in the Vedas the term Rishi means "the seer of the truth of the Mantras", and not any Brahmin with the holy thread hanging down the neck. The division of society into castes came about later on. Veda is of the nature of Shabda or of idea. It is but the sum total of ideas. Shabda, according to the old Vedic meaning of the term, is the subtle idea, which reveals itself by taking the gross form later on. So owing to the dissolution of the creation the subtle seeds of the future creation become involved in the Veda. Accordingly, in the Puranas you find that during the first Divine Incarnation, the Minâvatâra, the Veda is first made manifest. The Vedas having been first revealed in this Incarnation, the other creative manifestations followed. Or in other words, all the created objects began to take concrete shape out of the Shabdas or ideas in the Veda. For in Shabda or idea, all gross objects have their subtle forms. Creation had proceeded in the same way in all previous cycles or Kalpas. This you find in the Sandhyâ Mantra of the Vedas:

सूर्याचन्द्रमसौ धाता यथापूर्वमकल्पयत् पृथिवीं दिवं चान्तरीक्षमथो स्वः

— The Creator projected the sun, the moon, the earth, the atmosphere, the heaven, and the upper spheres in the same manner and process as in previous cycles." Do you understand?

Disciple: But, sir, how in the absence of an actual concrete object can the Shabda or idea be applied and for what? And how can the names too be given at all?

Swamiji: Yes. that is what on first thought seems to be the difficulty. But just think of this. Supposing this jug breaks into pieces; does the idea of a jug become null and void? No. Because, the jug is the gross effect, while the idea, "jug", is the subtle state or the Shabda-state of the jug. In the same way, the Shabda-state of every object is its subtle state, and the things we see, hear, touch, or perceive in any manner are the gross manifestations of entities in the subtle or Shabda-state. Just as we may speak of the effect and its cause. Even when the whole creation is annihilated, the Shabda, as the consciousness of the universe or the subtle reality of all concrete things, exists in Brahman as the cause. At the point of creative manifestation, this sum total of causal entities vibrates into activity, as it were, and as being the sonant, material substance of it all, the eternal, primal sound of "Om" continues to come out of itself. And then from the causal totality comes out first the subtle image or Shabda-form of each particular thing and then its gross manifestation. Now that causal Shabda, or word-consciousness, is Brahman, and it is the Veda. This is the purport of Sayana. Do you now understand?

Disciple: No, sir, I can't clearly comprehend it.

Swamiji: Well, you understand, I suppose, that even if all the jugs in the universe were to be destroyed, the idea or Shabda, "jug", would still exist. So if the universe be destroyed — I mean if all the things making up the universe be smashed to atoms — why should not the ideas or Shabdas representing all of them in consciousness, be still existing; And why cannot a second creation be supposed to come out of them in time?

Disciple: But, sir, if one cries out "jug", "jug", that does not cause any jug to be produced!

Swamiji: No, nothing is produced if you or I cry out like that; but a jug must be revealed if the idea of it rises in Brahman which is perfect in Its creative determinations. When we see even those established in the practice of religion (Sâdhakas) bring about by will-power things otherwise impossible to happen, what to speak of Brahman with perfect creativeness of will? At the point of creation Brahman becomes manifest as Shabda (Idea), and then assumes the form of "Nâda" or "Om". At the next stage, the particular Shabdas or ideas, that variously existed in former cycles, such as Bhuh, Bhuvah, Svah, cow, man, etc., begin to come out of the "Om". As soon as these ideas appear in Brahman endowed with perfect will, the corresponding concrete things also appear, and gradually the diversified universe becomes manifest. Do you now understand how Shabda is the source of creation?

Disciple: Yes, I just form some idea of it, but there is no clear comprehension in the mind.

Swamiji: Well, clear comprehension, inward realisation, is no small matter, my son. When the mind proceeds towards self-absorption in Brahman, it passes through all these stages one by one to reach the absolute (Nirvikalpa) state at last. In the process of entering into Samadhi, first the universe appears as one mass of ideas; then the whole thing loses itself in a profound "Om". Then even that melts away, even that seems to be between being and non-being. That is the experience of the eternal Nada. And then the mind becomes lost in the Reality of Brahman, and then it is done! All is peace!

The disciple sat mute, thinking that none could express and explain it in the way Swamiji was doing, unless the whole thing were a matter of one's own experience!

Swamiji then resumed the subject: Great men like Avatâras, in coming back from Samadhi to the realm of "I" and "mine", first experience the unmanifest Nada, which by degrees grows distinct and appears as Om, and then from Omkâra, the subtle form of the universe as a mass of ideas becomes experienced, and last, the material universe comes into perception. But ordinary Sadhakas somehow reach beyond Nada through immense practice, and when once they attain to the direct realisation of Brahman, they cannot again come back to the lower plane of material perception. They melt away in Brahman, "क्षीरे नीरवत् — Like water in milk".

When all this talk on the theory of creation was going on, the great dramatist, Babu Girish Chandra Ghosh, appeared on the scene. Swamiji gave him his courteous greetings and continued his lessons to the disciple.

Shabdas are again divided into two classes, the Vedic Shabdas and those in common human use. I found this position in the Nyâya book called *Shabdashaktiprakâshikâ*. There the arguments no doubt indicate great power of thought; but, oh, the terminology confounds the brain!

Now turning to Girish Babu Swamiji said: What do you say, G. C.? Well, you do not care to study all this, you pass your days with your adoration of this and that god, eh?

Girish Babu: What shall I study, brother? I have neither time nor understanding enough to pry into all that. But this time, with Shri Ramakrishna's grace, I shall pass by with greetings to your Vedas and Vedanta, and take one leap to the far beyond! He gets you through all these studies, because he wants to get many a thing done by you. But we have no need of them. Saying this, Girish Babu again and again touched the big Rig-Veda volumes with his head, uttering, "All Victory to Ramakrishna in the form of Veda!"

Swamiji was now in a sort of deep reverie, when Girish Babu suddenly called out to him and said: Well, hear me, please. A good deal of study you have made in the Vedas and Vedanta, but say, did you find anywhere in them any way for us out of all these profound miseries in the country, all these wailings of grief, all this starvation, all these crimes of adultery, and the many horrible sins?

Saying this he painted over and over again the horrid pictures of society. Swamiji remained perfectly quiet and speechless, while at the thought of the sorrows and miseries of his fellow men, tears began to flow out of his eyes, and seemingly to hide his feelings from us, he rose and left the room.

Meanwhile, addressing the disciple, Girish Babu said: Did you see, Bângâl? What a great loving heart! I don't honour your Swamiji simply for being a Pundit versed in the Vedas; but I honour him for that great heart of his which just made him retire weeping at the sorrows of his fellow beings.

The disciple and Girish Babu then went on conversing with each other, the latter proving that knowledge and love were ultimately the same.

In the meantime, Swamiji returned and asked the disciple, "Well, what was all this talk going on between you?" The disciple said, "Sir, we are talking about the Vedas, and the wonder of it is that our Girish Babu has not studied these books but has grasped the ultimate truths with clean precision!"

Swamiji: All truths reveal themselves to him who has got real devotion to the Guru; he has hardly any need of studies. But such devotion and faith are very rare in this world. He who possesses those in the measure of our friend here need not study the Shastras. But he who rushes forward to imitate him will only bring about his own ruin. Always follow his advice, but never attempt to imitate his ways.

Disciple: Yes, sir,

Swamiji: No saying ditto merely! Do grasp clearly the words I say. Don't nod assent like a fool to everything said. Don't put implicit faith, even if *I* declare something. First clearly grasp and then accept. Shri Ramakrishna always used to insist on my accepting every word of his only after clear comprehension of it. Walk on your path, only with what sound principle, clear reasoning, and scripture all declare as true. Thus by constant reflection, the intellect will become dear, and then only can Brahman be reflected therein. Do you understand?

Disciple: Yes, sir, I do. But the brain gets puzzled with the different views of different men. This very moment I was being told by Girish Babu, "What will you do with all this studying?" And then you come and say, "Reflect on what you hear and read about." So what exactly am I to do?

Swamiji: Both what he and I have advised you are true. The only difference is that the advice of both has been given from different standpoints. There is a stage of spiritual life where all reasonings are hushed; "मूकास्वादनवत् — Like some delicious taste enjoyed by the dumb". And there is another mode of spiritual life in which one has to realise the Truth through the pursuit of scriptural learning, through studying and teaching. You have to proceed through studies and reflection, that is *your* way to realisation. Do you see?

Receiving such a mandate from Swamiji, the disciple in his folly took it to imply Girish Babu's discomfiture, and so turning towards him said: "Do you hear, sir? Swamiji's advice to me plainly is just to study and reflect on the Vedas and Vedanta."

Girish Babu: Well, *you* go on doing so; with Swamiji's blessings, you will, indeed, succeed in that way.

Swami Sadananda arrived there at that moment, and seeing him, Swamiji at once said, "Do you know, my heart is sorely troubled by the picture of our country's miseries G. C. was depicting just now; well, can you do anything for our country?"

Sadananda: Mahârâj, let the mandate once go forth; your slave is ready.

Swamiji: First, on a pretty small scale, start a relief centre, where the poor and the distressed may obtain relief and the diseased may be nursed. Helpless people having none to look after them will be relieved and served there, irrespective of creed or colour, do you see?

Sadananda: Just as you command, sir.

Swamiji: There is no greater Dharma than this service of living beings. If this Dharma can be practiced in the real spirit, then "मुक्तिः करफलायते — Liberation comes as a fruit on the very palm of one's hand".

Addressing Girish Babu now, Swamiji said, "Do you know, Girish Babu, it occurs to me that even if a thousand births have to be taken in order to relieve the sorrows of the world, surely I will take them. If by my doing that, even a single soul may have a little bit of his grief relieved, why, I will do it. Well, what avails it all to have only one's own liberation? All men should be taken along with oneself on that way. Can you say why a feeling like this comes up foremost in my mind?

Girish Babu: Ah, otherwise why should Shri Ramakrishna declare you to be greater than all others in spiritual competence?

Saying this, Girish Babu took leave of us all to go elsewhere on some business.

X

(Translated from Bengali)
(From the Diary of a Disciple)

(The disciple is Sharatchandra Chakravarty, who published his records in a Bengali book, *Swami-Shishya-Samvâda*, in two parts. The present series of "Conversations and Dialogues" is a revised translation from this book. Five dialogues of this series have already appeared in the *Complete Works*, Vol. V.)

[Place: The Alambazar Math. Year: 1897.]

After Swamiji's first return to Calcutta from the West, he always used to place before the zealous young men who visited him the lofty ideals of renunciation, and anyone expressing his desire of accepting Sannyasa would receive from him great encouragement and kindness. So, inspired by his enthusiasm some young men of great good fortune gave up their worldly life in those days and became initiated by him into Sannyasa. The disciple was present at the Alambazar Math the day the first four of this batch were given Sannyasa by Swamiji.

Often has the disciple heard it from the Sannyasins of the Math that Swamiji was repeatedly requested by his brother-monks not to admit one particular candidate into Sannyasa, whereupon Swamiji replied: "Ah, if even *we* shrink from working out the salvation of the sinful, the heavy-laden, the humiliated, and the afflicted in soul, who else are to take care of them in this world? No, don't you please stand against me in this matter." So Swamiji's strong opinion triumphed, and always the refuge of the helpless, he resolved out of his great love to give him Sannyasa.

The disciple had been staying at the Math for the last two days, when Swamiji called him and said: "Well, you belong to the priestly class; tomorrow you get them to perform their Shrâddha, and the next day I shall give them Sannyasa. So get yourself ready by consulting the books of ceremonials today." The disciple bowed this mandate of Swamiji, and the ceremony was duly gone through.

But the disciple became very much depressed at the thought of the great sternness of Sannyasa. Swamiji detecting his mental agitation asked him, "Well, I see, you feel some dread in your mind at all this experience, is it not so?" And when the disciple confessed it to be so Swamiji said: "From this day these four are dead to the world, and new bodies, new thoughts, new garments will be theirs from tomorrow — and shining in the glory of Brahman they will live like flaming fire! 'न कर्मणा न प्रजया धनेन त्यागेनैके अमृतत्वमानशुः — Not by work, nor by progeny, nor by wealth, but by renunciation alone some (rare ones) attained Immortality' (Kaivalya Upanishad)."

After the ceremony, the four Brahmacharins bowed at the feet of Swamiji. He blessed them and said, "You have the enthusiasm to embrace the loftiest vow of human life; blessed indeed is your birth, blessed your family, blessed the mothers who held you in their womb! 'कुलं पवित्रं जननी कृतार्या — The whole family-line becomes hallowed, the mother achieves her highest!'"

That day after supper, Swamiji talked of the ideal of Sannyasa alone. To the zealous candidates for Sannyasa, he said: The real aim of Sannyasa is " आत्मनो मोक्षार्थं जगद्धिताय च — For one's highest freedom and for the good of the world". Without having Sannyasa none can really be a knower of Brahman — this is what the Vedas and the Vedanta proclaim. Don't listen to the words of those who say, "We shall both live the worldly life and be knowers of Brahman." That is the flattering self-consolation of cryptopleasure-seekers. He who has the slightest desire for worldly pleasures, even a shred of some such craving, will feel frightened at the thought of the path you are going to tread; so, to give himself some consolation he goes about preaching that impossible creed of harmonising Bhoga and Tyâga. That is all the raving of lunatics, the frothing of the demented — idle theories contrary to the scriptures, contrary to the Vedas. No freedom without renunciation. Highest love for God can never be achieved without renunciation. Renunciation is the word — "नान्यः पन्था विद्यते अयनाय — There's no other way than this." Even the Gita says, "काम्यानां कर्मणां न्यासं संन्यासं कवयो विदुः — The sages know Sannyasa to be the giving up of all work that has desire for its end."

Nobody attains freedom without shaking off the coils of worldly worries. The very fact that somebody lives the worldly life proves that he is tied down to it as the bond-slave of some craving or other. Why otherwise will he cling to that life at all? He is the slave either of lust or of gold, of position or of fame, of learning or of scholarship. It is only after freeing oneself from all this thraldom that one can get on along the way of freedom. Let people argue as loud as they please, I have got this conviction that unless all these bonds are given up, unless the monastic life is embraced, none is going to be saved, no attainment of Brahmajnâna is possible.

Disciple: Do you mean, sir, that merely taking up Sannyasa will lead one to the goal?

Swamiji: Whether the goal is attained or not is not the point before us now. But until you get out of this wheel of Samsâra, until the slavery of desire is shaken off, you can't attain either Bhakti or Mukti. To the knower of Brahman, supernatural powers or prosperity are mere trivialities.

Disciple: Sir, is there any special time for Sannyasa, and are there different kinds of it?

Swamiji: There is no special time prescribed for a life of Sannyasa. The Shruti says: "यदहरेव विरजेत् तदहरेव प्रवजेत् — Directly the spirit of renunciation comes, you should take to Sannyasa." The *Yogavâsishtha* also says:

युवैव धर्मशील: स्यात् अनित्यं खलु जीवितम् ।
को हि जानाति कस्याद्य मृत्युकालो भविष्यति ॥

— "Owing to life itself being frail and uncertain, one should be devoted to religion even in one's youth. For who knows when one's body may fall off?"

The Shâstras are found to speak of four kinds of Sannyasa: (1) Vidvat, (2) Vividishâ, (3) Markata, (4) Âtura. The awakening of real renunciation all at once and the consequent giving up of the world through Sannyasa is something that never happens unless there are strong Samskâras or tendencies, developed from previous birth. And this is called the Vidvat Sannyasa. Vividisha Sannyasa is the case of one who, out of a strong yearning for the knowledge of the Self through the pursuit of scriptural study and practice, goes to the man of realisation and from him embraces Sannyasa to give himself up to those pursuits. Markata Sannyasa is the case of a man who is driven out of the world by some of its chastisements such as the death of a relative or the like and then takes to Sannyasa, though in such a case the renouncing spirit does not endure long. Shri Ramakrishna used to say of it, "With this kind of renunciation one hastens away to the up-country and then happens to get hold of a nice job; and then eventually perhaps arranges to get his wife brought over to him or perhaps takes to a new one!" And last, there is another kind of Sannyasa which the Shastras prescribe for a man who is lying on his death-bed, the hope of whose life has been given up. For then, if he dies, he dies with the holiest of vows upon him, and in his next birth the merit of it will accrue to him. And in case he recovers, he shall not go back to his old life again but live the rest of his days in the noble endeavour after Brahmajnana. Swami Shivananda gave this kind of Sannyasa to your uncle. The poor man died; but through that initiation he will come to a new birth of higher excellence. After all there is no other way to the knowledge of the Self but through Sannyasa.

Disciple: What then, sir, will be the fate of the householders?

Swamiji: Why, through the merit of good Karma, they shall have this renunciation in some future birth of theirs. And directly this renunciation comes, there is an end of all troubles — with no further delay he gets across this mystery of life and death. But then all rules have their exceptions. A few men, one or two, may be seen to attain the highest freedom by the true fulfilment of the householder's Dharma, as we have amongst us Nâg Mahâshaya, for instance.

Disciple: Sir, even the Upanishads etc. do not clearly teach about renunciation and Sannyasa.

Swamiji: You are talking like a madman! Renunciation is the very soul of the Upanishads. Illumination born of discriminative reflection is the ultimate aim of Upanishadic knowledge. My belief, however, is that it was since the time of Buddha that the monastic vow was preached more thoroughly all over India, and renunciation, the giving up of sense-enjoyment, was recognised as the highest aim of religious life. And Hinduism has absorbed into itself this Buddhistic spirit of renunciation. Never was a great man of such renunciation born in this world as Buddha.

Disciple: Do you then mean, sir, that before Buddha's advent there was very little of the spirit of renunciation in the country, and there were hardly any Sannyasins at all?

Swamiji: Who says that? The monastic institution was there, but the generality of people did not recognise it as the goal of life; there was no such staunch spirit for it, there was no such firmness in spiritual discrimination. So even when Buddha betook himself to so many Yogis and Sâdhus, nowhere did he acquire the peace he wanted. And then to realise the Highest he fell back on his own exertions, and seated on a spot with the famous words, " इहासने शुष्यतु मे शरीरं — Let my body wither away on this seat" etc., rose from it only after becoming the Buddha, the Illumined One. The many monasteries that you now see in India occupied by monks were once in the possession of Buddhism. The Hindus have only made them their own now by modifying them in their own fashion. Really speaking, the institution of Sannyasa originated with Buddha; it was he who breathed life into the dead bones of this institution.

Swami Ramakrishnananda, a brother-disciple of Swamiji, interposed, "But the ancient law-books and Puranas are good authority that all the four Ashramas had existed in India before Buddha was born." Swamiji replied, "Most of the Puranas, the codes of Manu and others, as well as much of the

Mahâbhârata form but recent literature. Bhagavân Buddha was much earlier than all that." "On that supposition," rejoined Swami Ramakrishnananda, "discussions about Buddhism would be found in the Vedas, Upanishads, the law-books, Puranas, and the like. But since such discussions are not found in these ancient books, how can you say that Buddha antedated them all? In a few old Puranas, of course, accounts of the Buddhistic doctrine are partially given; but from these, it can't be concluded that the scriptures of the Hindus such as the law-books and Puranas are of recent date."

Swamiji: Please read history, (Evidently, during the argumentation, Swamiji was taking his stand on the conclusions of modern historical studies, thereby giving his encouragement and support to such new efforts and methods. But we know from one of his letters to Swami Swarupananda (C.W. Vol. V,) that Swamiji broke off later on from the position of these modern scholars and worked out the pre-Buddhistic origin of much of modern Hinduism.) and you will find that Hinduism has become so great only by absorbing all the ideas of Buddha.

Swami Ramakrishnananda: It seems to me that Buddha has only left revivified the great Hindu ideas, by thoroughly practicing in his life such principles as renunciation, non-attachment, and so on.

Swamiji: But this position can't be proved. For we don't get any history before Buddha was born. If we accept history only as authority, we have to admit that in the midst of the profound darkness of the ancient times, Buddha only shines forth as a figure radiant with the light of knowledge.

Now the topic of Sannyasa was resumed and Swamiji said: Wheresoever might lie the origin of Sannyasa, the goal of human life is to become a knower of Brahman by embracing this vow of renunciation. The supreme end is to enter the life of Sannyasa. They alone are blessed indeed who have broken off from worldly life through a spirit of renunciation.

Disciple: But many people are of opinion nowadays, sir, that with the increase of wandering monks in the country, much harm has been done to its material progress. They assert it on the ground that these monks idly roam about depending on householders for their living, that these are of no help to the cause of social and national advancement.

Swamiji: But will you explain to me first what is meant by the term material or secular advancement?

Disciple: Yes, it is to do as people in the West are doing by securing the necessaries of life through education, and promoting through science such objects in life as commerce, industry, communications, and so on.

Swamiji: But can all these be ever brought about, if real Rajas is not awakened in man? Wandering all over India, nowhere I found this Rajas manifesting itself. It is all Tamas and Tamas! The masses lie engulfed in Tamas, and only among the monks could I find this Rajas and Sattva. These people are like the backbone of the country. The real Sannyasin is a teacher of householders. It is with the light and teaching obtained from them that householders of old triumphed many a time in the battles of life. The householders give food and clothing to the Sadhus, only in return for their invaluable teachings. Had there been no such mutual exchange in India, her people would have become extinct like the American Indians by this time. It is because the householders still give a few morsels of food to the Sadhus that they are yet able to keep their foothold on the path of progress. The Sannyasins are not idle. They are really the fountain-head of all activity. The householders see lofty ideals carried into practice in the lives of the Sadhus and accept from them such noble ideas; and this it is that has up till now enabled them to fight their battle of life from the sphere of Karma. The example of holy Sadhus makes them work out holy ideas in life and imbibe real energy for work. The Sannyasins inspire the householders in all noble causes by embodying in their lives the highest principle of giving up everything for the sake of God and the good of the world, and as a return the householders give them a few doles of food. And the very disposition and capacity to grow that food develops in the people because of the blessings and good wishes of the all-renouncing monks. It is because of their failure to understand the deeper issues that people blame the monastic institution. Whatever may be the case in other countries, in this land the bark of householders' life does not sink only because the Sannyasins are at its helm.

Disciple: But, sir, how many monks are to be found who are truly devoted to the good of men?

Swamiji: Ah, quite enough if one great Sannyasin like Shri Ramakrishna comes in a thousand years! For a thousand years after his advent, people may well guide themselves by those ideas and ideals he leaves behind. It is only because this monastic institution exists in the country that men of his greatness are born here. There are defects, more or less, in all the institutions of life. But what is the reason that in spite of its faults, this noble institution stands yet supreme over all the other institutions of life? It is because the true Sannyasins forgo even their own liberation and live simply for doing good to the world. If you don't feel grateful to such a noble institution, fie on you again and again!

While speaking these words, Swamiji's countenance became aglow. And before the eyes of the disciple he shone as the very embodiment of Sannyasa.

Then, as if realising deep within his soul the greatness of this institution, self-absorbed, he broke forth in sweetest symphony:

"वेदान्तवाक्येषु सदा रमन्तो
भिक्षान्नमात्रेण च तुष्टिमन्तः ।
अशोकमन्तःकरणे चरन्तः
कौपीनवन्तः खलु भाग्यवन्तः ॥

— "Brooding blissful in mind over the texts of the Vedanta, quite contented with food obtained as alms and wandering forth with a heart untouched by any feeling of grief, thrice blessed are the Sannyasins, with only their loin-cloth for dress."

Resuming the talk, he went on: For the good of the many, for the happiness of the many is the Sannyasin born. His life is all vain, indeed, who, embracing Sannyasa, forgets this ideal. The Sannyasin, verily, is born into this world to lay down his life for others, to stop the bitter cries of men, to wipe the tears of the widow, to bring peace to the soul of the bereaved mother, to equip the ignorant masses for the struggle for existence, to accomplish the secular and spiritual well-being of all through the diffusion of spiritual teachings and to arouse the sleeping lion of Brahman in all by throwing in the light of knowledge. Addressing then his brothers of the Order, he said: Our life is "आत्मनो मोक्षार्थं जगद्धिताय च — for the sake of our self-liberation as well as for the good of the world". So what are you sitting idle for? Arise, awake; wake up yourselves, and awaken others. Achieve the consummation of human life before you pass off — "Arise, awake, and stop not till the goal is reached."

XI

(Translated from Bengali)

(From the Diary of a Disciple)

(The disciple is Sharatchandra Chakravarty, who published
his records in a Bengali book, *Swami-Shishya-Samvâda*, in two
parts. The present series of "Conversations and Dialogues" is a
revised translation from this book. Five dialogues of this series
have already appeared in the *Complete Works*, Vol. V.)

*[Place: The house of the late Babu Navagopal Ghosh, Ramakrishnapur, Howrah,
6th February, 1898.]*

Today the festival of installing the image of Shri Ramakrishna was to
come off at the residence of Babu Navagopal Ghosh of Ramakrishnapur,
Howrah. The Sannyasins of the Math and the householder devotees of Shri
Ramakrishna had all been invited there.

Swamiji with his party reached the bathing ghat at Ramakrishnapur.
He was dressed in the simplest garb of ochre with turban on his head and
was barefooted On both sides of the road were standing multitudes of
people to see him. Swamiji commenced singing the famous Nativity Hymn
on Shri Ramakrishna — "Who art Thou laid on the lap of a poor Brahmin
mother", etc., and headed a procession, himself playing on the Khol. (A
kind of Indian drum elongated and narrows at both ends.) All the devotees
assembled there followed, joining in the; chorus.

Shortly after the procession reached its destination, Swamiji went
upstairs to see the chapel. The chapel was floored with marble. In the centre
was the throne and upon it was the porcelain image of Shri Ramakrishna.
The arrangement of materials was perfect and Swamiji was much pleased
to see this.

The wife of Navagopal Babu prostrated herself before Swamiji with the
other female members of the house and then took to fanning him. Hearing
Swamiji speaking highly of every arrangement, she addressed him and
said, "What have we got to entitle us to the privilege of worshipping Thâkur
(the Master, Lord)? — A poor home and poor means! Do bless us please by
installing him here out of your own kindness!

In reply to this, Swamiji jocosely said, "Your Thakur never had in his fourteen generations such a marble floored house to live in! He had his birth in that rural thatched cottage and lived his days on indifferent means. And if he does not live here so excellently served, where else should he live?" Swamiji's words made everybody laugh out.

Now, with his body rubbed with ashes and gracing the seat of the priest, Swamiji himself conducted the worship, with Swami Prakashananda to assist him. After the worship was over, Swamiji while still in the worship-room composed extempore this Mantra for prostration before Bhagavan Shri Ramakrishna:

$$\text{"स्थापकाय च धर्मस्य सर्वधर्मस्वरूपिणे}$$
$$\text{अवतारवरिष्ठाय रामकृष्णाय ते नमः ॥}$$

— "I bow down to Ramakrishna, who established *the* religion, embodying in himself the reality of all religions and being thus the foremost of divine Incarnations."

All prostrated before Shri Ramakrishna with this Mantra. In the evening Swamiji returned to Baghbazar.

XII

(Translated from Bengali)

(From the Diary of a Disciple)

(The disciple is Sharatchandra Chakravarty, who published his records in a Bengali book, *Swami-Shishya-Samvâda*, in two parts. The present series of "Conversations and Dialogues" is a revised translation from this book. Five dialogues of this series have already appeared in the *Complete Works*, Vol. V.)

[Place: Balaram Babu's residence, Calcutta. Year: 1898.]

Swamiji had been staying during the last two days at Balaram Babu's residence at Baghbazar. He was taking a short stroll on the roof of the house, and the disciple with four or five others was in attendance. While walking to and fro, Swamiji took up the story of Guru Govind Singh and with his great eloquence touched upon the various points in his life — how the revival of the Sikh sect was brought about by his great renunciation, austerities, fortitude, and life-consecrating labours — how by his initiation he re-Hinduised Mohammedan converts and took them back into the Sikh community — and how on the banks of the Narmada he brought his wonderful life to a close. Speaking of the great power that used to be infused in those days into the initiates of Guru Govind, Swamiji recited a popular Dohâ (couplet) of the Sikhs:

"सवा लाख पर एक चढाऊं।
जब गुरुगोविन्द नाम सुनाऊं॥

The meaning is: "When Guru Govind gives the Name, i.e. the initiation, a single man becomes strong enough to triumph over a lakh and a quarter of his foes." Each disciple, deriving from his inspiration a real spiritual devotion, had his soul filled with such wonderful heroism! While holding forth thus on the glories of religion, Swamiji's eyes dilating with enthusiasm seemed to be emitting fire, and his hearers, dumb-stricken and looking at his face, kept watching the wonderful sight.

After a while the disciple said: "Sir, it was very remarkable that Guru Govind could unite both Hindus and Mussulmans within the fold of his religion and lead them both towards the same end. In Indian history, no other example of this can be found."

Swamiji: Men can never be united unless there is a bond of common interest. You can never unite people merely by getting up meetings, societies, and lectures if their interests be not one and the same. Guru Govind made it understood everywhere that the men of his age, be they Hindus or Mussulmans, were living under a regime of profound injustice and oppression. He did not create any common interest, he only pointed it out to the masses. And so both Hindus and Mussulmans followed him. He was a great worshipper of Shakti. Yet, in Indian history, such an example is indeed very rare.

Finding then that it was getting late into the night, Swamiji came down with others into the parlour on the first floor, where the following conversation on the subject of miracles took place.

Swamiji said, "It is possible to acquire miraculous powers by some little degree of mental concentration", and turning to the disciple he asked, "Well, should you like to learn thought-reading? I can teach that to you in four or five days."

Disciple: Of what avail will it be to me, sir?

Swamiji: Why, you will be able to know others' minds.

Disciple: Will that help my attainment of the knowledge of Brahman?

Swamiji: Not a bit.

Disciple: Then I have no need to learn that science. But, sir, I would very much like to hear about what you have yourself seen of the manifestation of such psychic powers.

Swamiji: Once when travelling in the Himalayas I had to take up my abode for a night in a village of the hill-people. Hearing the beating of drums in the village some time after nightfall, I came to know upon inquiring of my host that one of the villagers had been possessed by a Devatâ or good spirit. To meet his importunate wishes and to satisfy my own curiosity, we went out to see what the matter really was. Reaching the spot, I found a great concourse of people. A tall man with long, bushy hair was pointed out to me, and I was told that person had got the Devata on him. I noticed an axe being heated in fire close by the man; and after a while, I found the red-hot thing being seized and applied to parts of his body and also to his hair! But wonder of wonders, no part of his body or hair thus branded with the red-hot axe was found to be burnt, and there was no expression of any pain in his face! I stood mute with surprise. The headman of the village, meanwhile, came up to me and said, "Mahâraj, please exorcise this man out of your mercy." I felt myself in a nice fix, but moved to do something, I had to go near the possessed man. Once there, I felt a strong impulse to examine the axe rather closely, but the instant I touched it, I burnt my fingers, although the thing had been cooled down to blackness. The smarting made me restless and all my theories about the axe phenomenon were spirited away from my mind! However, smarting with the burn, I placed my hand on the head of the man and repeated for a short while the Japa. It was a matter of surprise to find that the man came round in ten or twelve minutes. Then oh, the gushing reverence the villagers showed to me! I was taken to be some wonderful man! But, all the same, I couldn't make any head or tail of the whole business. So without a word one way or the other, I returned with my host to his hut. It was about midnight, and I went to bed. But what with the smarting burn in the hand and the impenetrable puzzle of the whole affair, I couldn't have any sleep that night. Thinking of the burning axe failing to harm living human flesh, it occurred again and again to my mind, "There are more things in heaven and earth, Horatio, than are dreamt of in your philosophy."

Disciple: But, could you later on ever explain the mystery, sir?

Swamiji: No. The event came back to me in passing just now, and so I related it to you.

He then resumed: But Shri Ramakrishna used to disparage these supernatural powers; his teaching was that one cannot attain to the supreme truth if the mind is diverted to the manifestation of these powers. The layman mind, however, is so weak that, not to speak of householders, even ninety per cent of the Sâdhus happen to be votaries of these powers. In the West, men are lost in wonderment if they come across such miracles. It is only because Shri Ramakrishna has mercifully made us understand the evil of these powers as being hindrances to real spirituality that we are able to take them at their proper value. Haven't you noticed how for that reason the children of Shri Ramakrishna pay no heed to them?

Swami Yogananda said to Swamiji at this moment, "Well, why don't you narrate to our Bângâl (Lit. A man from East Bengal, i.e. the disciple.) that incident of yours in Madras when you met the famous ghost-tamer?"

At the earnest entreaty of the disciple Swamiji was persuaded to give the following account of his experience:

Once while I was putting up at Manmatha Babu's (Babu Manmatha Nath Bhattacharya, M.A., late Accountant General, Madras.) place, I dreamt one night that my mother had died. My mind became much distracted. Not to speak of corresponding with anybody at home, I used to send no letters in those days even to our Math. The dream being disclosed to Manmatha, he sent a wire to Calcutta to ascertain facts about the matter. For the dream had made my mind uneasy on the one hand, and on the other, our Madras friends, with all arrangements ready, were insisting on my departing for America immediately, and I felt rather unwilling to leave before getting any news of my mother. So Manmatha who discerned this state of my mind suggested our repairing to a man living some way off from town, who having acquired mystic powers over spirits could tell fortunes and read the past and the future of a man's life. So at Manmatha's request and to get rid of my mental suspense, I agreed to go to this man. Covering the distance partly by railway and partly on foot, we four of us — Manmatha, Alasinga, myself, and another — managed to reach the place, and what met our eyes there was a man with a ghoulish, haggard, soot-black appearance, sitting close to a cremation ground. His attendants used some jargon of South Indian dialect to explain to us that this was the man with perfect power over the ghosts. At first the man took absolutely no notice of us; and then, when we were about to retire from the place, he made a request for us to wait. Our Alasinga was acting as the interpreter, and he explained the requests to us. Next, the man commenced drawing some figures with a pencil, and presently I found him getting perfectly still in mental concentration. Then he began to give out my name, my genealogy, the history of my long line of forefathers and said that Shri Ramakrishna was keeping close to me all through my wanderings, intimating also to me good news about my mother. He also foretold that I would have to go very soon to far-off lands for preaching religion. Getting good news thus about my mother, we all travelled back to town, and after arrival received by wire from Calcutta the assurance of mother's doing well.

Turning to Swami Yogananda, Swamiji remarked, "Everything that the man had foretold came to be fulfilled to the letter, call it some fortuitous concurrence or anything you will."

Swami Yogananda said in reply, "It was because you would not believe all this before that this experience was necessary for you."

Swamiji: Well, I am not a fool to believe anything and everything without direct proof. And coming into this realm of Mahâmâya, oh, the many magic mysteries I have come across alongside this bigger magic conjuration of a universe! Maya, it is all Maya! Goodness! What rubbish we have been talking so long this day! By thinking constantly of ghosts, men become ghosts themselves, while whoever repeats day and night, knowingly or unknowingly, "I am the eternal, pure, free, self-illumined Atman", verily becomes the knower of Brahman.

Saying this, Swamiji affectionately turned to the disciple and said, "Don't allow all that worthless nonsense to occupy your mind. Always discriminate between the real and the unreal, and devote yourself heart and soul to the attempt to realise the Atman. There is nothing higher than this knowledge of the Atman; all else is Maya, mere jugglery. The Atman is the one unchangeable Truth. This I have come to understand, and that is why I try to bring it home to you all. " — "एकमेवाद्वयं ब्रह्म", "नेह नानास्ति किञ्चन" "One Brahman there is without a second", "There is nothing manifold in existence" (Brihadâranyaka, IV. iv. 19)

All this conversation continued up to eleven o'clock at highs. After that, his meal being finished, Swamiji retired for rest. The disciple bowed down at his feet to bid him good-bye. Swamiji asked, "Are you not coming tomorrow?"

Disciple: Yes, sir, I am coming, to be sure. The mind longs so much to meet you at least once before the day is out.

Swamiji: So good night now, it is getting very late.